GREEN CARD LOTTERY and The American Dream

KENYAN WINNER SURPRISES, APPREHENSION AND EXPERIENCES

by

John K. Kananda, Unity in Diversity Ministry

**1622 W. University Dr. Ste B/525
DENTON, TX 76201**

authorHOUSE®

AuthorHouse™
1663 Liberty Drive, Suite 200
Bloomington, IN 47403
www.authorhouse.com
Phone: 1-800-839-8640

True story in essence but the teller requested her real name not be used to avoid drawing attention to her family who live in Kenya. Consequently her name and all other real names in the story have been changed.

First published by AuthorHouse 12/11/2007

ISBN: 978-1-4343-5390-0 (e)
ISBN: 978-1-4343-5389-4 (sc)

Library of Congress Control Number: 2007909608

Printed in the United States of America
Bloomington, Indiana

This book is printed on acid-free paper.

INTRODUCTION

What is Green Card Lottery?

Green Card lottery, also known as Diversity Visa (DV) Lottery, is a category of immigrants program administered on annual basis by the U.S. Department of State under the terms of Section 203(c) of the Immigration and Nationality Act (INA). The Act makes available 50,000 permanent resident visas annually to persons from countries with low rates of immigration to the United States. To be included in the lottery, applicants have to meet simple, but strict, eligibility requirements. Selection is by computer and eligible applicants have equal chances of being picked.

Many people who are interested, and would qualify, fail to apply partly because they do not have adequate information how the program is administered but mainly because private businesses who are not affiliated to U.S. Government charge a fee for services and expertise.The fact is that the application is **free** for anyone with a computer and connection to the internet. You can submit own application at home, in a public library or at a computer internet café by logging to the USCIC website www.dvlottery.state.gov. After careful review of current instructions the applicant should complete an entry form which is online. Those who do not have the time, access to a computer and/or expertise may resort to the commercial agents for help with the application. In this regard, both the United States Department of State and the Federal Trade Commission have issued warnings for consumers to look out for fraud in this or similar business practices.

Selected applicants may not be aware that there will be a lengthy waiting period before one is invited for interview. The interview itself is not a walkover. While most of those who get to the interview get visas after verification of eligibility requirements, some do not get interview invitations after all because of **quota** and **time** limiting factors.

Global and country quota

The annual quota is 50,000 visas world wide but the computer selects about twice as many apparent qualifiers because some will be disqualified for various reasons including failure to prove claimed eligibility requirements. Once the world quota is met no further interviews are held for that program. There is a country quota too. The world is divided into six regions and rules say within each region, no one country may receive more than seven percent of the available Diversity Visas in any one year.

Time factor

The visa issuing period for every annual program is announced at the time of release. As an example, DV2009 opened October 3 until December 2, 2007. Selection is May to July 2008 and interviews shall be January 1 to September 30, 2009. There are no further interviews or redemption of unclaimed visas for this program after that date. You can see complete DV2009 instructions at : http://travel.state.gov/pdf/2009DVInstructions.pdf

Those selected by computer and families, where applicable, are interviewed and on passing have to pay a predetermined visa fee. Currently DV Lottery surcharge for immigrant visa application (per person applying as a result of the lottery program) is $375.00. Other expenses follow including travel to United States, room and food while waiting for legal documments to arrive and the entire process of securing gainful employment. It is important for those seeking green card visas to understand that the U.S. Government does not cover these costs.

As if this is not overwhelming enough, new immigrants have to adjust to American culture and work ethic. Every green card immigrant has a story to tell. The stories range from comfy to downright horrendous depending on where the immigrant is coming from in terms of exposure and experience, their expectations, their hosts, adaptability etc.

What follows is a totally true story as told by Martha, a brave Kenyan girl, who won green card at a tender age of 18 years with just high school diploma, no work or travel experience and limited resources. This is her "learn as you go" experience and, I believe, it mimics that of many other USA new immigrants in same or similar situation. Unity in Diversity is authoring this story in the context of our goal to empower potential and new USA legal immigrants through sharing and exchange of information.

Martha met many people in Kenya, after being selected in the lottery program, who claimed to know USA very well. Unfortunately, they gave conflicting reports about the country and she did not know who to believe. She shares her own experience after relocation and attempts to explain why people have different views about America.

Those people who hosted Martha after arrival played a major role in inspiring her to an early experience of the American Dream. Another great resource was a booklet entitled Welcome to the United States: A Guide for New Immigrants published by the United States Center for Immigration Service (USCIS). The complete guide is accessible online at the USCIS website: http://www.uscis.gov/. For the sake of those to who internet is not readily available, we have copied the text from four sections that Martha found most helpful in Appendix III. They are listed below.
- Getting settled in the United States
- Education and Childcare
- Learning about United States of America AND
- Becoming a U.S. Citizen

Unity in Diversity Ministry is a Community Based Organization (CBO) whose mission is to empower disadvantaged communities through sharing and exchange of information. One of our projects is engaged in counseling USA new legal immigrants. The target group is prospective and newly landed immigrants and the goal is to make their relocation and assimilation in local communities as easy and as soon as possible. For more information on the organization visit www.uidministry.com or write to:

The Director
Unity in Diversity Ministry
1622 W. University Dr. Ste B/525
Denton, Tx 76201

Life changing action

I had just turned 18, had a High School diploma and no job or possibility for further education when my girlfriend Lisa Kimani and I walked to Maxus Internet café on 4th floor of Kenya National Union of Teachers (KNUT) House in Nairobi, to apply for green card to come to America. I will never forget that day. It was Tuesday 23rd December 2003. Lisa and I met while attending a hair dressing training college in Westlands where we were enrolled six months earlier from different backgrounds. My dad enrolled me at the college because he believed the course would enhance my chances of securing employment. In the event that I did not get a job, he would raise some capital for me to start a business and become self-employed. Lisa on the other hand came from a better off family and was sponsored by her auntie so that she can be attending to their children whenever they needed hair to be done. Motivation to apply for green card on this day was influenced by a casual visit Lisa and I made to her relatives who live in Buruburu housing estate the previous night. This is how it had played out.

The day was Monday 22nd December in the afternoon. Lisa and I had not planned to meet but we happened to be at the premises of our former college at the same time. Each had come to pick up their certificate because our course had ended previous week.

Lisa and I go visiting

Lisa and I lived in South B. She invited me to accompany her as she was going to visit her relatives that afternoon. The first born in the family we were going to visit, who goes by the name Darius Njenga, had won green card in 1999 and had lived in America since. According to Lisa, Darius was gone only three years but he had elevated the family from the poverty line to what can be considered wealthy in Kenyan standards. We arrived early in the evening and we were well received. We joined other girls in the kitchen and assisted in preparing supper. There was joy and laughter from 'girls talk' as they were catching up with each other because Lisa had not visited the family for a while.

4

At the dinner table Lisa asked the parents how Darius was doing in America. They talked freely about his accomplishments in my presence because they knew I was Lisa's friend and posed no threat to the family. They explained how their son works hard and sends them money to meet their needs and to invest. "There are so many opportunities for work in America" Darius had written recently, one can work round the clock if it was humanly possible". While on this subject we talked about employment in our job market. One girl said employers no longer advertise jobs in Kenya for fear of being swamped with applications. Most of jobs advertised in the newspapers were by government departments. It was suggested these advertisements are just a formality because the jobs are filled long before they appear in the paper. There was laughter in the room when someone else said if the boss did not have someone in mind to fill a vacancy it is because no opening exists.

Fewer jobs, higher education
To shield children from frustration parents who can afford send them for higher education even when they have a first degree. This has resulted in too many degreed people who cannot find even jobs that are comfortably done by persons with high school education. As a high school graduate, that statement left me scared. I wondered if employers are hiring degreed workers for jobs meant for us. What then shall we do with our certificates? I wished my parents could afford to send me back to school for higher studies. I was tired waiting for a job that was not forthcoming. This discussion ended but it became the beginning of my thoughts about America. I was beginning to be crazy about relocating to America where finding work is not a problem so that I can support my family as Darius has done.

As we were going home, I asked Lisa to tell me more about Darius and another friend she had in America. I had gotten to know Darius name that night but there was another guy she had been talking about. She reminded me his name: Joakim Karemi and he was Darius roommate. They lived in Dallas, Texas. Lisa had introduced Darius to Joakim because he, Joakim, had gone to the USA in 1998. This was the start of yet another very interesting discussion. I wanted Lisa to have Darius and Joakim invite us to join them in America.

Securing visitor visa was hard

I asked Lisa why she had not made any effort to join Joakim and Darius in USA. She said she would tell me what she did not like sharing with people, even close friends, because it was embarrassing. She had applied for visitor visa several times at the Embassy and each time she was denied. The third and last time she appeared for interview was 2002. They said she is not allowed to reapply for at least another year because her circumstances were not different from previous applications. After that she was disillusioned. She had spent a lot of money and energy preparing for those interviews and could not imagine appearing at that Embassy any more. "I hate their guts" She said. I got a sense of her frustration and did not want her to talk about her experience any more. I asked her if she had ever applied for green card and she said she had never. The fact that it is called lottery made her feel like it was a 'long shot'. She did not think she was the lucky type as had been demonstrated by her failure to secure visitor visa three times. This response was not convincing to me. If Darius made it, we can!

Please place that call

It was still early in the evening when we got at Lisa's home. I prevailed on her to call Joakim or Darius so that they can tell us more about the green card program. We placed the call and hang up so that they could call us back Lisa told me she just sends a flash signal or email message because it is expensive to call from Kenya and they call her back. Due to time difference it was early morning in their part of USA and we found Joakim at home. He was taking a break from work that day. We talked for about an hour from 11.00pm to some time after midnight. Both Lisa and I took turns on the phone. When it was my turn to talk to him, he told me winning green card lottery was a legal way of relocating to America. At my insistence Joakim went into details how the green card program works and said he was encouraged that we were preparing to apply. The merits of this type of visa are that those selected from the lottery are neither required to produce proof of substantial financial resources nor do they need to prove how connected they are to their country of residence through employment and/or family. These two requirements, according to him, were the main stumbling blocks to those who apply for visitor visa. The Consular Officers who process these applications treat everyone as potential immigrant and the onus is on the applicant to prove otherwise. This is a very difficult task. Approval does not just depend on having all the required information and a healthy bank account. You can still be denied and their decision is final.

Green card was the way to go

Given my great desire to have a job and to pursue higher education, this information made me even more determined to try my luck at the green card lottery program. Downside of the green card lottery program, according to Joakim, was that it takes months for winners to be notified while losers receive no communication at all. The program that was open at that time was DV2005. With closing date only six days away, he said we must hurry. I told Lisa we had to submit our applications the next day.

I spent the night at Lisa's house because it was too late to go home. I left for home very early because I was to accompany my parents to our rural home to celebrate Christmas with extended family. Lisa was doing the same but we agreed to pass by the internet café mentioned earlier at noon. The Manager was a young man who was very proficient in using his computer. He explained the process, requirements and the applicable fee. We posed for digital photographs, answered to a questionnaire as he did some maneuvers behind the machine and within minutes he printed confirmations that our applications were received in USA. What was the cost? Kenyan Shillings 1,000. - ($15 at the time). Honestly I thought it was a rip off but Lisa comforted me by saying the management at the café was reliable and that the same job would have cost more elsewhere. Both of us used Lisa's address because they collected mail from post office regularly.

My first surprise

Weeks and months passed. Lisa and I talked about many things except about winning green card lottery to go to America. Then one evening in May 2004, after we had forgotten we applied for green card, Lisa came across a letter addressed to me in their mail box and rushed it to me. The letter started with the words "Congratulations, you have been selected……." It was all joy and screams as we danced around in the house. Initially I thought I could start saying goodbye to family and friends and hop on the plane within days but on reading further I noticed this was the beginning of another process. It was a notification that I had been selected for interview to determine whether I was qualified to be granted a green card to go to America. There was no indication when the interview would be. However, the letter had a dire warning that I should not quit my job, assuming I had one, or sell my property until the interview happens and I am granted the green card. Memories went back to the visit Lisa and I made to Darius parents in Buruburu. The interest I put in at the time had started to pay dividends. Neither Lisa nor I had found jobs yet and I believed Darius was still over there in the USA working as much as he wanted and supporting his family.

One month, two, three and many more passed without further communication. Just as Joakim made me aware, it took time before one is invited for interview but he also said some people end up not being invited at all. I was worried about the letter getting lost in the post office, because they do, and also my age. They could have reviewed the application again and decided to disqualify me because I was too young. Lisa's case was even worse. She had not received a selection notice and at this time she had to forget about green card during the current year.

Another pleasant surprise

My letter for interview finally arrived in May 2005, twelve months after the selection notice. The interview was scheduled to take place at the American Embassy in Gigiri on July 25, 2005 at 8.30am. I was required to bring with me a Certificate of Good Conduct from the Police, a medical report, certificates as proof of my academic achievements, sixty five thousand Kenyan Shillings ($1,000 at the time) and affidavit of support or proof that I had adequate financial resources to cover my travel and initial expenses while in USA for a couple of months before getting a job. They also asked me to provide a name and physical address of someone who would be my host on arrival. A list of doctors approved to carry out the medical examination was attached. They said the cost depended on the doctor but on average I should expect to spend about eleven thousand Kenyan Shillings.

Preparing for my interview
While I was happy to attend interview, I decried the listed expenditure items. First, there was no guarantee that after spending this money I would pass the interview. Second, I had to go back to my parents for support because I was unemployed. Lisa and I discussed my concerns at length and we concluded I had to find a way of financing the interview and subsequent expenses and repay the money when I start working in USA. Strategizing further, we decided to convene a small meeting with my parents and siblings to discuss the money issue.

The meeting took place one week later. Everyone we invited attended and they were very excited. Everyone expected me to pass the interview and the general talk was how they were going to miss me when I am gone. My dad preempted discussing expenses leading to the interview by stating he had the money I needed. It was a big relief and we shifted to other things that needed to be done before the interview. He also surprised everyone by disclosing something he had never told me or anyone else in the family including mum. He said when I was young he had a dream about me going to far places and he thought his dream was coming true at this time.

Looking beyond the interview, dad said he was planning to sell some properties to cover other expenses associated with my travel. This made me uncomfortable because I did not want him to spend any more money on me. We had three sisters in school and they needed his support more than I did. I told him Lisa and I had a plan to look for someone to finance my expenses and I would repay the money with interest while working in America. We decided to focus only on what had to be accomplished before the interview. We developed a list of thing to be done and shared the tasks amongst ourselves as follows:

- I was to collect my High School certificate from former school, Certificate of Good Conduct from Criminal Investigation Department Headquarters and then call around for a doctor from the provided list to book for medical examination.
- Lisa was going to contact Darius and Joakim for their physical and email addresses as well as assurance of initial support on my arrival.
- My dad was going to talk to a family friend, Joyce, to become my supporter and I would refund any money she advanced within a reasonable time when I started working in USA.
- Joyce was to be requested to obtain statements from her bank, to accompany her own letter of support which I would present to the Embassy during the interview.

The next day, I started at CID Headquarters to collect Certificate of Good Conduct. They asked me for my national identification card (id) and I told them I did not have one yet. They said I needed a letter of identification from my former school and Shs.500.00 fee. When I returned in the afternoon with the letter they took my fingerprints and asked me to come for the report after seven days. From there I was on my way home when I paused: "Wait a minute; I need to have a passport at the interview. We overlooked this at the meeting last night. How do I get one?"

Passport would not be guaranteed
In the afternoon I went to the Kenyan Immigration Department to enquire about getting the passport urgently because I needed it for the interview. The first thing they wanted from me was my (id). That just sent a chill down my spine because if they insisted on id I would not get one for months to come. However, they accepted the letter from former school which I had obtained for the CID Headquarters. The second question was why I needed the passport.

I showed them a letter inviting me for interview and they gave me application forms. They said I should return the completed forms with the required fee and warned me it takes about three months to process a passport. They would therefore not guarantee that I was going to get it in good time for my interview.

I left feeling discouraged. Shall I miss a golden opportunity because my Government which cannot give me a job after school will not process a passport for me to move to America, a country that is inviting me to go and work? If I knew someone in high place, I would probably get my passport within days. Now that I do not, I may not get it in months or at all. While this was going on in my mind, I recalled reading about an anti-corruption unit based in the same building as the immigration department and I decided to stop at their office to ask for help. The lady I found at the reception desk listened intently and she was very sympathetic. She asked me to come back next day with the completed forms and the necessary fee and she would follow up and make sure I get my passport in good time for the interview. I did as she advised.

Miracles begin to happen
Four days later, I received a call from the immigration department asking me to go and pick up my passport. Halleluiah! This shocked me any many people because passports take months and sometimes up to a year to be issued. The clerk who gave me the passport would not look at me on the face. She was present when I was told it would take three months and I think they received a directive from their boss to process it immediately.

Meanwhile, my dad had talked to Joyce, the family friend, and she agreed to advance money I needed for travel and other expenses if I passed the interview. She called her bank and asked them to prepare bank statements for pick up the next day. Halleluiah!

After raising the money required for the interview, obtaining a passport and gathering my certificates, the medical exam was now the major hurdle between me and the American Embassy. What was required before the doctor would certify me fit to go to America? I would soon find out.

At the doctor's clinic I was presented with a questionnaire about my health and that of my immediate family. They took my vital signs and blood samples before I was ushered into the doctor's room. The doctor asked me more questions and then examined me from head to toe. No part of my body was spared. I asked the doctor why the questionnaire was gathering information about my family. Would they get visas too? He said they asked such questions to guide them on what tests they should carry out. It had nothing to do with the family. On the way out, I was given a bill of ten thousand shillings. After payment they said a copy of my report would be mailed directly to the Embassy but I should collect the original after one week. It would be marked confidential and addressed to the Consular Section at the Embassy.

One day before the interview, I picked up the report. It was another moment of anxiety since I was aware I was carrying the results of the first test to determine whether I would pass or fail the interview and I had no way of telling whether it was positive or negative.

On the eve of the interview, my dad gathered the immediate family again, including Lisa, for a prayer meeting. What was facing me, he said, was a life changing event. He went on to pour praises about my organized life since I was a young child to an extent where my sisters began to show signs of jealousy. He recounted how my teachers in both Primary and High School had persistently reported my performance as excellent in both academic and extra-curricular activities. Given this track record, he had no doubt I would carry the same personality and attitude to the interview and when in America I would succeed beyond many people's expectation. He concluded with a prayer for God to bless events of the next day and every day thereafter.

That evening I did a final checklist of the things I was required to bring to the Embassy including Certificate of Good Conduct from the Police, my passport, medical report, High School certificate, affidavit of support and the name and physical address of the person to receive me in America.

The Interview

July 25, 2005. - is the day I had been preparing for. I was apprehensive and nervous. What kind of questions do they ask? Does it take the form of job interview or is it more like an interrogation? Shall I be required to write anything?

I arrived at the Embassy in good time and passed through the security detail to the waiting room. Everybody in the room appeared to be in suspense and they were also carrying envelops with reports and I presume documents. Those who were presenting themselves for interview as a family talked in low tones but all others, including me, were silent with eyes transfixed toward the interview counters. At exactly 8.30 am three service windows opened. They were labeled by the type of interview to take place at the respective window as follows:

- Visitors
- Students
- Green Card

Names started to be called out at each window. Some people were interviewed only for short time while others took much longer. As one would expect, my attention was at the green card window. From the distance, I could not tell the nature of discussion but I watched as conversation and documents were exchanged between the officer and interviewees and finally the person being interviewed left with either a happy or gloomy face. A few did not show any emotion and it was hard to tell whether they got what they wanted or not. The officer appeared courteous but serious with what she was doing. Their facial expressions did not show anything other than business as usual. As I sat waiting, I thought about my family and what they had gone through to help me prepare for this interview. I had no experience in interviews since I had not interviewed for a job since leaving school. Yet here I am expected to put in my best for me and my family, so help me God! At about 10.30 am, two hours after arrival at the waiting room, my name was called out. My stomach went jelly and my legs felt weak as I walked to the counter.

The interviewer: "Good morning Martha Ny......How do you pronounce the last name?"
My response: "Good morning to you. My last name is pronounced Nya-mbu-ra"
She smiled and this made me feel encouraged. I offered to hand over all the documents in my possession but she said: "Thank you but hold on to those documents for now and pass them to me in the order of relevance to my questions. Does that make sense?" She asked.
I replied that it makes sense and then she started the interview.

First she asked me for my passport, Certificate of Good Conduct and then the medical report. There was a pause as she opened the report and studied it and then put it aside. "May I see your High School or other certificates please?" she asked.

As she was scrutinizing my certificate, she asked me what my favorite subject in school was to which I replied geography. This prompted a follow up question to name the five largest cities in the State of New York. I named New York City , Buffalo, Rochester, Yonkers, and ....?. I struggled to remember the fifth but she said that was good enough. As she was making her notes, I started to wander into possible areas of further questioning. I reminded myself the names of some of the states in USA in case she posed that question. I could remember New York, since we had just mentioned it, Texas, New Jersey, California, Mississippi, Indiana, Kansas, Louisiana, Maryland and Florida. I imagined her saying ten out of fifty should be good enough. Then I switched to civics. The current President is George W Bush. Yes, the one with W as middle name because the other is the father who is now former president. However, her questioning took a different direction as follows:

"How are you going to finance your travel and initial expenses in America?" She asked.

Without saying a word I gave her a healthy bank statement from Joyce which was certified by her bank. "If we grant you a visa do you have a name and address of someone who will receive you and help you to settle in America?" She continued. I handed to her an email from Darius with the required information. There being no other questions, she asked me to come back on 4th August to pick up my passport stamped with the visa.

It was such a relief to pass the interview after two months of preparation and suspense. It was time to reflect on the questions and my answers. I do not think I could have done better. After all I passed the interview and that is what matters. The city that had escaped my memory was now available – <u>Syracuse</u>.

I walked out of the Embassy premises with a sigh of relief since I carried good news to my family and friends.

Celebration with tears of joy
My dad and sisters had braved the long wait outside the Embassy. When they saw me leave the gate their heads were raised and ears open to receive the news. Unfortunately, I could not hold my emotions and when I got close to them I collapsed at my dad's feet before saying a word and cried uncontrollably. They were confused because they did not know why I was crying and they led me to a waiting car and we headed home. When I regained my normal self after about ten minutes I told them the good news and now it was my sisters' turn to cry with joy. My dad started praying and thanking God for His blessings to me and the family.

Travel within six months or forfeit my visa
On August 4, 2005, I picked up my passport from the Embassy. I also received a sealed letter addressed to the Immigration which I was supposed to deliver personally at the point of entry within six months or forfeit my green card. This was yet new information to me about the green card process. I was hoping I would hold on to the visa and stay with my family as long as I wanted and then leave for America at my convenience. I was later to learn that America's

different types of visas carry different rights and privileges. There is more about this in Appendix I of this book.

Working with a Travel Agent
Another first in my life was the visit to a travel agent to check on availability of flights and the cost involved. My hosts in America told me to tell the agent the day I was expected to arrive at DFW Airport in Dallas, Texas, which is the day they were available to pick me up. A travel plan would evolve showing date of departure and the routing. This encounter taught me a lot about international travel including:
- Generally, cost of travel is affected by distance and the time of year one travels.
- There are low seasons and high seasons and cost of tickets move accordingly.
- Irrespective of the season, direct flights are more expensive than flights with connections or stopovers.
- If one is going overseas for a visit, they are required to buy a two way or return ticket which is valid for one year. However, green card holders and students may buy one way ticket because they are not expected to return within one year.
- The cost of one way ticket is not half the return ticket. It is about 80%. This is probably how airlines recoup the cost of empty seats since planes travel by schedule even if they are not full.

Budget for my support
The travel plan that my dad and I favored was to start from Nairobi on October12, by a flight called the Emirates and travel through Dubai to London where I would catch a connecting flight to USA. The flight from London would take me to Houston, Texas, and then connect by another domestic flight to Dallas where I would arrive on October 13. This one way economy class ticket cost Kenyan Shillings ninety thousand ($1,500.-).

Lisa's friends who were going to meet me at the DFW airport approved the plan and offered to do whatever it would take to get me settled in the United States as soon as possible after arrival and at minimum cost. Their strategy was to shield me from having to spend money on some of what they called "big spenders" in the first few months but I would need some pocket money to meet my basic needs. They listed the big spenders during the first six months as:

1. Rent and utilities
2. Food and clothing
3. Taking driving lessons
4. Training to become a CNA
5. Motor vehicle for driving to work

Their contribution was to cover items 1-3 for a couple of months during which I would enroll and complete Certified Nursing Assistant (CNA) class, get a job and then proceed to rent my own apartment.

Out of my pocket expenses for the six months was estimated at $500. - I needed $800 to pay for CNA class and $2,200 down payment for a used car. There was also the cost of my ticket and when we did the math it came to $5000. – This was the budget my dad was going to present to Joyce.

Joyce response was positive because she had confidence in me and trusted my dad. She gave us a check for the full amount we requested and asked us to schedule repayment of the same amount within 24 months. She did not charge us interest. This was great help.

Conflicting reports about navigating life in America
I was amazed at the attention I was receiving since I got a visa to USA. Family and friends became friendlier and people I did not know before wanted us to be acquaintances. The main theme of discussion was life in USA. Some people had visited or knew a family or friend who was or had been there. Their opinions ranged from life in America being excellent to despondent. A balancing voice in this sea of conflicting views came from Lisa and her friends in America. Joakim, had this to say about the differing views:

"If you can make it in Africa, you will excel in USA. If you cannot make it in Africa you will get lost in America. Beware; those who talk about America negatively" he continued "may be recycling the story of the rabbit. When the rabbit could not reach some deep red grapes he said it does not matter anyway because after all they are bitter. When you come to America, work hard; enroll in classes to study and stay focused. Keep good company and avoid anyone who would lead you to engage in self destructive activities."

After listening to Joakim I thought I was beginning to have an answer why I was hearing so many stories of great success punctuated by few stories of failure. Many Kenyans are hard working at home and abroad. As far as I am concerned I was confident I can make it in Africa and therefore encouraged that I will excel when I go to America.

My dad had encouraging words too. He compared the divergent views of opinion to the proverbial elephant and ten blind men. They were asked to move to the elephant briefly, touch it and then come back and describe what they thought the elephant was like. On return, those who touched the side said it was like a big playing field; those who touched the trunk said it was like a big teapot with a mighty exhaust etc. Similarly, America is a big country constituting fifty states in a wide spread geographical area. Those who go to the north will say America is biting cold in winter; those who go to Southern states like Texas will say it is deadly hot in summer. Some states have to deal with drug trafficking more than others and some have to deal with gangs. He said while in America, I should endeavor to do that which is legal at all times, be professional and flexible and all other things will take care of themselves. He concluded with a message from James 1:17.

Family separation was going to be painful.
Time was moving very fast for me. I felt bad that I was leaving my mum, dad and sisters to a far country and wished I could stay longer with them before departing. On the other hand it was easy for me to wind up my life in Kenya because I was single; I had no job to

quit and no assets to sell. Considering what I had gone through as an individual I could imagine how hectic and expensive it is for families who go through this process.

Lisa remained my closest confidant on my travel arrangements and future plans. We decided it was not necessary to share the information beyond the family except for Edith who wanted to come to the airport to see me off. Meanwhile hosting arrangements in USA were complete and it was time to leave.

JKIA Airport …on your Mark...Get ready…set and Go!

It was the morning of October 12, 2005 when most of my family, young and old, came to the airport to see me off. Lisa was there too and a few close friends especially from the Church. The family came in a minibus and the others in personal cars. I was humbled to see this spectacle created just for me. I said a silent prayer that my travel to America would be worthwhile and that I would make them all proud when they see my success.

Saying goodbye was the hardest thing that I had done in my life to date. My mother was by my side as I moved from one relative or friend to the next for a brief hug and to hear words of comfort and encouragement. My nephew was only six then and he screamed when he was told they came to the airport to say farewell to me because I was leaving by plane to a far country. Finally my dad gathered us all in a circle and I stepped in the middle. He read a passage from the Bible and those who could reach me put their hands on me as he said a moving prayer. I felt more vulnerable than I had felt at any time before but I remained composed.

It was two hours to departure time and my dad and brother in law moved my luggage to the check-in counter. The clerk behind the counter asked for my passport and ticket. She asked if the luggage was to be checked all the way to destination at the DFW Airport in Dallas and we said that was fine. Looking at me, she asked me to make sure all my basic needs on the way were in the carry on bag because I would not have access to my luggage during stopovers in

Dubai and London. I think she suspected I was a first time traveler and may not be familiar with such regulations. She pulled two out of the four coupons in the ticket and put them in separate pouches labeled "Boarding Pass". She explained one was to be used for the current flight to Dubai and the other for the Dubai/London flight. The remaining coupons were for the London/Houston and Houston/DFW. She gave back to me the passport, ticket and boarding passes and directed me through a gate marked 'passengers only'. At the gate I waved for the last time to everybody and I disappeared.

There was a queue in front of me and a counter marked immigration. As I approached the counter the officer asked me for my passport, ticket and boarding pass. He stamped the passport "JKA Exit October 12, 2005" and handed it back to me with ticket and boarding pass. It was no longer getting ready; it was getting set to go!

Departing Kenya
I took an elevator to the first floor and found myself in the departure lounge. There were many people waiting for flights to different places. The airport view was much better here and I could see many planes and various activities around the airport like loading cargo, servicing planes, arriving, and departing passengers etc. I walked about in the lounge and saw duty free shops, money exchange bureaus, restaurants and rest rooms. Departure gates had numbers and I waited at the gate marked on my boarding pass until the flight to Dubai was called to board.

I am boarding the plane
Everything happened just as I had seen in the movies and therefore I did not need to ask any questions. Our hand luggage went though a screening machine and we had a body check before proceeding into a tunnel that led us to the plane cabin. I followed the seat rows to the number allocated to me per the boarding pass. The overhead storage was too far up for me but there was a cabin crew ready to help me with that. When everyone was on board and seated, the doors were closed and announcements began. The flight attendant, speaking on behalf of the Captain and crew, welcomed us on board.

She apologized for the slight delay caused by the plane arriving late. I really did not know the plane was late because I did not have an idle moment.

Thereafter we rolled out of the parking and headed for the runway. My seat was next to a window and when the plane started rolling forwards, I closed my eyes and preferred to feel rather than to see what was going on. Five minutes later I felt some calm and opened my eyes and saw white clouds below. Moments later there was an announcement that we could undo our seat belts and there were clicks all over the plane. There were more announcements from the cabin and crew about the weather on route, the time it would take to Dubai, meal schedule etc.

Mistaken for naïve
It did not take me long to discover there were many young people on the flight because they started walking up and down the aisle. Some looked like students returning from vacation in Kenya. The person sitting next to me was not young. It was a middle aged man and I could see he was anxious to start a conversation. A moment presented itself when suddenly the plane started shaking and jerking and I was terrified. When he noticed this, he asked me if I was a first time traveler to which I replied in the affirmative. He then started to explain that we were going through an air pocket and that there was nothing to worry about. He told me he was a frequent traveler and this time he was heading to Tokyo for business.

I replied to this guys question guardedly because my dad had warned me not to tell too much about myself to strangers and to seek guidance and directions only from uniformed personnel. I told him I was coming to the United States and he suggested I must be coming to study to which I said yes. He wanted to know the name of the State I was headed to and the name of College and I told him I had relatives waiting for me at the other end and since I have never been to USA before I did not have those details. When I told him I was landing at DFW Airport he knew it was in Texas and he told me about many friends he had in the State and other places in USA.

Just before we landed in Dubai he came up with what he thought was a "brilliant" idea. He wanted to change his travel plan to pass through DFW airport and then catch a connecting flight to Tokyo so that he could ensure my safety. This would entail me stopping in Dubai too to give him a chance to go to the travel agent to change his ticket. Was this not a conman? You bet. He thought I was naïve but he was very wrong. I pretended to be nice to him by urging him not to go through such inconvenience and expense for me but to give me his contact so that I can keep in touch when I get to USA. I made sure he did not see my full name and/or address. As soon as he was out of my sight, he was out of my mind. By the way, I do remember him telling me his name but it did not register in my mind. He said he comes from Sudan and he has business interests in Nairobi, Kampala and Mombasa. As for the paper he wrote the name and address, there was no second guessing. I trashed it soon after embarking from the plane.

Not again?!?... Did I just look simple and vulnerable?
The waiting time at Dubai airport was brief. As we embarked, transport was available to whisk us to another Emirate connecting flight to London. One young man who was in the previous flight introduced himself as Benson from Ndeiya but he and his parents have a farm in Limuru. When I told him my name he beamed. We just discovered we were both Kikuyu and conversation continued in vernacular. He offered to carry my hand luggage to the waiting vehicle and I obliged. There was a lot of excitement and he too wanted to know where I was heading to and what I was going to do. He said he had taken notice of me since JKA airport in Nairobi where he saw me in a group that had come to see me off. His onward flight from London was to New York and then he would go by road to New Jersey. He asked to see my ticket and I could not deny him because it was on my hand and he could see it. He commented in sort of disappointment that his flight was by different carrier at different time from London. He wished we could fly from London together because he thought I was a good girl. From his face expressions and these remarks, I knew I was out for another experience.

Benson was not about to let me have my way any more, at least up to London. He appeared to be a well experienced traveler because when he read my boarding pass he said our seats were seven rows apart. I did not know how he could tell those small details but I did not want to ask else he would know I have no travel experience. When we went to board the flight he told the attendant we were together and that we should be given adjacent seats. She said the seats were allocated in Nairobi and there was nothing she could do at that time. We had to take the seats as pre-allocated. Benson appeared the kind of person who had to have what he wants or nothing. I am scared of such guys and I was glad we were in public place. Anyway, he said as soon as we were airborne he would look for two empty seats which were together and we should move there. The take off from Dubai was not as smooth as JKA in Nairobi. It took a long time for the plane to stabilize and for a while it felt like we were going back to land. As soon as the seatbelt sign went off, Benson was by my side pointing at some place where we were going to move to. I told him I was feeling nauseated like I could vomit and needed sometime to get better before moving about. He came back after five minutes and told me he had persuaded his neighbor to move instead and that I should move to that seat. He removed my hand luggage from the overhead closet and we moved to his row and sat together. He was very happy and I was very scared but I held myself as if everything was fine.

This was the time to share information about ourselves. He asked me to tell him about me and I told him he was the one to start and he did. He was educated in Nyeri High School and then went to Egerton College where he got a degree in Agriculture Engineering. He could not get a job in the field he trained in and he took up a teaching job at a high school in Nakuru before his father got him a scholarship to study Veterinary Science at a University in USA. I asked him how life was in USA as compared to Kenya and he told me so much in such short time that I could write another book. In short he said USA is many countries that have come together under one Government and one culture. It is the strongest country in the world economically and militarily. They do not have much regard for degrees earned in foreign countries and especially Africa. One has to acquire American education to receive recognition. With or without high education, reward is proportional to hard work. If the announcement to prepare for landing did not come, he would have gone on and on. I was happy that there was no time to tell my history. I said since we are both in America, we shall find a way of continuing our discussion and he was very happy about that. He gave me his address and phone number and asked me to call him the next day after I arrive. He said he was prepared to come to Texas and meet my relatives if that was ok with me.

Benson's flight was departing from Heathrow but I had to change airport to Gatwick. It was therefore goodbye and with a possibility of seeing you later. There was a six hour waiting period at Gatwick. I was very tired and all I did was lean back on a platform and take a nap.

Trans-Atlantic Flight
The flight from Gatwick to Houston was at night. I had an aisle seat and sat next to a newly wed couple who were returning from honey moon in England. They were so much into each other that we did not say more than hello. After dinner and a movie the lights were turned off and most of the people slept.

I was unable to sleep because my mind was going back and forward. Every flight was taking me further away from my loving parents, siblings and other relatives. The people I was going to meet in Texas were not known to me in any way other than name. What kind of people are they? Am I going to be safe over there? I bought one way ticket and it cost a lot of money. What if I feel unsafe and I want to go back home? Benson said Americans do not have much regard for certificates acquired from foreign countries. Will they accept my High School certificate for employment? How does one apply for a job?

No turning back! America is my new found country for better or worse.

It was about 10.00am on October 13, 2005 when the plane landed at Houston airport. This being an incoming international flight we were all required to clear through the Immigration. I passed on the sealed envelop that was given to me at the American Embassy to the Immigration and the next thing the Officer said was "Welcome to America." Those words were refreshing considering the physical and emotional torture I had gone through. I was directed to a side office where some paperwork had to be processed. I thought it was just routine one page document followed by stamping of my passport as happened in Dubai and London. However, this was to be another interview just as had happened at the Embassy in Nairobi except the questions were different. I was asked to identify myself and explain how I had received the sealed envelope. Luckily I had kept all my documents intact from the letter of selection to the letter inviting me for interview. I was then given forms to apply for a social security card and the green card. Thereafter my passport was tamped with one year multiple entry visa which I could use to travel out of the country anytime before receiving the green card. They also said I would be receiving a social security card in the mail between two and three weeks but the green card would take much longer. I was going to be a Permanent Resident!

Missed connecting flight

The welcome process took about one hour. The flight I was expected to take to DFW airport in Dallas took off without me. I raised the issue with the office where I was being attended and they said I should not worry because there were several flights on my route in the course of the day. I could not verbalize my feeling but there was no way I could stop worrying because there were people waiting for me at the other airport and I did not know how to communicate this information. As a first time traveler, it would have been nice to stick to my schedule to avoid inconveniencing other people. Anyway, before I left the office they booked me on the next available flight which was to leave at 3.45pm.

The DFW flight took off on time at 3.45pm and it took only 30 minutes before a voice from the cockpit said we were preparing to land. With no immigration procedures to clear it was from the plane to luggage collection area. I scanned through the waiting crowd looking for a familiar face. I had met Darius briefly in Nairobi in 2004 when he came on vacation and he had a parcel to deliver to Lisa from Joakim. I was expecting both Darius and Joakim at the airport but I had never met Joakim.

I picked up my luggage from the conveyor belt and I stood there waiting when someone walked up to me and said "welcome to Dallas Margaret". It was Joakim. He noticed me from some photos he had received from Lisa. He said Darius was unable to stay at the airport because he had to go to work. With regard to the delay in Houston, he said he had called to confirm I was on the flight from London and understood why I missed the connecting flight. He told me it had been agreed with Lisa that I would go to stay with Darius. He and Darius were no longer roommates because he had moved to another city. Darius had also moved to live with another roommate.

The start of my life in Dallas
It was a long drive from the airport and there were great highways and many high-rise buildings on the way. I thought of Nairobi as compared to Dallas and it is but a "drop in the ocean".

Joakim turned off from main Highway 635 East to a street called Forest Lane. He said Darius lived in that location with a roommate but he was not familiar with the area. He called the apartment and we got directions how to get there from the roommate. Joakim told me her name was Teresia. When we arrived, she was home but Darius was still at work. She introduced herself and said I can call her Terry in short. Joakim consulted with Terry briefly and they told me I was going to be sleeping on the couch until I secured my own apartment. That was many months away because there were many things to do before I was ready to be on my own. The neighborhood had other Kenyans and some stopped by to check on Darius and Terry. They were happy to meet a new arrival from home. We chatted about many things including the latest developments in Kenya.

At about 9.00pm Joakim had to leave because he lived in Denton, fifty miles from Dallas, and he had to go to work at 11.00pm. I was beginning to be curious about working hours. They said Darius had gone to work at 2.00pm and would finish at 10.00pm. Joakim was going to work at 11.00pm and was going to finish at 7.00am the next day. I therefore raised the question about working hours in America. They said most foreigners are in Health and Entertainment sectors as well as security and the jobs in these sectors are 24 hours divided into 3 shifts of 8 hours each or 2 shifts of 12 hours each. It was also the practice of foreign workers to have two or more jobs in the same sector or across sectors. I did not need to ask why they do two or three jobs. Actually I looked forward to doing the same.

Darius arrived at about 10.30pm and found me still watching television because I was not feeling sleepy. I was happy to see him. He said he had come to the airport with Joakim at 11.00am but when the plane I was booked arrived I was no where to be seen. He had to leave because he was going to work.

Primary host has no time for me
The next morning, Darius and Terry left the apartment at 5.30am. Darius was working a double shift until 10.00pm and Terry was going for a 12 hour shift until 6.00pm. They said I should look in the refrigerator for food and drinks. They also showed me the stove and microwave if I wanted to cook or heat anything. I had not slept the whole night because my biological clock was telling me it was day as if I was in Kenya. I flipped TV channels all night with low volume, so as not to disturb Darius and Terry looking for Kenyan news but I did not find any. I was going to ask them how to access the news from Africa, and especially Kenya, but they left for work before I did that.

The day was quiet except for telephone calls. I had not asked my hosts about answering the phone but I decided to pick up the calls in case they were trying to reach me from their job. Most of the calls were about sale of products or holiday travel packages and I asked them to call later when the owners were in the house. Darius called mid morning to find out if I had any problems and I raised the issue of those calls. I learned the callers are called telemarketers and I should not waste my time talking to them. They said as soon as I hear them talking about sale of products, I should hang up. Personally, I thought it would be rude to hang up when someone is still trying to talk to me on the phone but I had to do as instructed by my hosts. Much later during my stay, I appreciated why they had to resort to this apparently rude behavior. With regard to news from Africa, they said it only happens if there is a great disaster that cannot be ignored. The American media is patriotic. They tell Americans what is going on in America as priority news and will occasionally talk about Europe, Asia and Latin America in as far as it is of interest to Americans or as "by the way" to top up their airtime if there were no advertisements.

Two weeks passed by with me sleeping and waking in the sitting room with the television as my only companion. Darius and Terry were hardly ever in the apartment at the same time. They were either at work, sleeping or hurriedly grabbing a snack on their way to work. I had many questions to settle with them and I was getting very frustrated because it looked as if they did not care. Joakim called several times because he had to keep Lisa informed about my welfare. I didn't tell him about my frustrations because I did not want to appear ungrateful to Darius and Terry. I asked Joakim why it was decided I should stay in Dallas and not Denton since it appeared as if he would have sometime for me. He said there were two considerations: First, Dallas is better served with public transportation than Denton. Since I did not have a car as yet I could still go about my normal business by train and the bus. Secondly, Darius and Terry as a couple would provide me a more homely atmosphere. He told me he had asked if I could go to Denton in the first place but Lisa and Darius insisted on Dallas. I asked if Terry was part of that decision and Joakim just laughed. He later told me jokingly, "Darius is just a paying guest in that apartment".

Darius and Terry found it convenient to sign for more working hours because when they arrived at home I had already cooked and cleaned the house. When they had sometime to spare it was to go to the store to buy groceries, do personal laundry and catch up with lost sleep. Meanwhile, I was losing time and the understanding reached between the hosts and Lisa was not being honored. On their part Darius and Terry said nothing could be done until I receive my social security card. While this was understandable they should take me out to places that I will be going to look for work when the social security card arrives. They just did not seem to care.

It was the fourth week with nothing happening and Joakim became concerned. He came to see Darius to arrange for me to go and do a live-in job in Denton while waiting to attend a CNA course that is offered for free by a local nursing home in exchange for signing to work for the facility for six months. Since there was no other plan laid out for me, Darius said he would drive me to Denton at the end of the week. Meanwhile Joakim was going to arrange for the job and the training opportunity.

Rescued by second host
It was on December 15, 2005, more than one month since arrival in Dallas, that Darius drove me to Denton. Joakim had arranged with an employee of a hiring Agency to pick me up at 4.00pm to take me to their client. I will refer to the client only as Sarah because I cannot disclose her real name. She was about 85 years old and could do many things on her own. She had cataract in both eyes and therefore partially blind and her hearing was also impaired. My main job was to keep her company, cook and give her medications at scheduled times. Her apartment had two bedrooms and I would occupy one of them. There was a TV in each bedroom and in the living room. There was also a computer with access to the internet 24/7. It was a very luxurious apartment. I spent that evening and the next day orienting with the outgoing employee. This was a better home. I did not have to sleep on the couch and I was going to be paid for cleaning and cooking.

On the job training begins

The nurse responsible for Sarah's health came to meet me and went over the medications that she takes. She told me why; how and when to give the medications. She also went over the documentation maintained and when to request for replenishment. It was also my duty to maintain a daily journal to record who visited and why and any other significant incidents that occur, the time they occur and how they are dealt with. Finally we went over the phone numbers of people to call and when to call and especially the emergency number 911. The emergency number was to be called first in case of a life threatening incident like a fire breakout, fall or choking. Thereafter I was to call the nurse, the family and the agency in that order.

The employee from the Agency returned next day with paper work to complete with regard to the job and to explain the terms of employment. The rate of pay was $8.25 but since I was living in for free half of the hours would go towards my own expenses. The fine details were rather complicated but the bottom line was that I would live with Virginia 24 hours a day for five days a week and in return get paid $500.=(Five hundred dollars) before taxation. If there was no one to work the other two days of the week, and I opt to work, I was going to be paid overtime at time and a half or $150.= per day. I thought I had been surprised but this was the real one. I had never been in an organization payroll since leaving school and if this is the start, the sky will be the limit. That feeling persisted until I started spending the money and discovered that the expenditure side had its own surprises too. I looked up the phone directory and called to make an appointment to have my hair done the following Saturday and the quote was $250. = for making simple lines on my head. But this is 50% of my weekly pay. What if I had started paying rent, buying food and paying utilities?

Training continues

Two days after the former employee left, Sarah's daughter came to visit her. She introduced herself and told me she was the legal guardian of her mother. She sat me down and we went over the same job description that I had covered with the nurse, former employee and the Agency representative. She noticed I had struck a very cordial relationship with her mother in the two days I worked there and it looked like it was going to get even better. She was very excited about this. The only thing we did not talk about was the pay because that was between me and the Agency.

After she left I started to figure out how I was going to relate with all the stake holders. Sarah being a high level client was giving me instructions, so was her daughter, the nurse and the Agency. If I got my way there were also some changes I would make in the house to give it a better look. Shall I have the freedom to do this? The issue was, who is my boss among the family, employer and the healthcare worker and what leeway did I have to use my initiative and previous experience?

Client is my boss
The answer to my question did not take long to be answered. The Agency employee returned the following week to deliver my check and wanted to know what my first week experience was. I told him I was very happy with the job and that Sarah was very happy too. He told me I should refer all questions of my employment such as days off, vacation and my duties to the Agency. The family is not allowed to change my duties without reference to the Agency. The nurse is also an employee of the Agency and we should work together to make sure Sarah was healthy, comfortable and secure. She is the one who pays our bills. Sarah is our boss!

Life lessons begin
My days at Sarah's were occupied by house work and keeping her company. She was very curious about my life history, my family and my country. She also told me a lot of things about herself, her family and about America. During her teenage years, America went through a very difficult economic period she referred to as "the great Depression". The depression had devastating effect on incomes due to widespread unemployment arising from closure of construction and other industries. Farming was also affected as crop prices fell drastically. In the 1940's American economy took an upward turn.

The fear of a repeat of depression made the government and the American people to pursue prudent fiscal policies ever since. The government keeps a close watch on inflation and unemployment statistics while regulating the money market through the interest rate adjustments. The population became savers not only for a rainy day but for retirement. The savings become investments and investments boost the economy hence employment.

With regard to inflation, she said the government mints and releases money into the economy to match people's capacity to produce goods and services. If for a given amount of money in circulation production drops without equivalent reduction of the money supply OR too much money is in cirgulation relating to the volume of goods and services THEN there is inflation. In other words, inflation is too much money chasing too few goods. This is a very common phenomena in collapsing economies in Africa. At one point in time, there was such high inflation in the Congo that you needed a seven ton load of their highest denomination note to buy a one ton truck. There is talk of something similar coming home in Zimbabwe. When I shared that information with Sarah she said that is the chronic part of inflation. It is called hyper inflation and the cure is withdrawal from money use and retun to barter or exchanging goods for goods.

I was very grateful to Sarah because this was my first lesson in economics. I decided to leave it at that until I take a class in College to learn more about the subject but in the mean time I was able to relate this explanation to the problems affecting developing countries like Kenya. Sarah may not have been aware but the issue of employment touched me the most. The greatest problem young people face is unemployment. Many are educated and very hard working but there are no jobs. America has jobs because of government intervention in the economy through the fiscal policies. Why doesn't our government do the same? I have noted as an example that the American government maintains and announces every month the rate of unemployment. In my country and many other developing contries, the government does not know at any time what the rate of unemployment is. It is usually given as a range between 30 and 50 percent. If you include the underemployed, then the figure jumps to about 70 to 80 percent.

Utilizing time wisely
In the evenings Sarah went to bed early and left me to watch television and read Kenyan news on the internet. I decided to spend this time also reading more about America since it is my new home. This would also help when talking to Sarah because she was asking me simple questions that I could not answer such as how big Kenya is compared to Texas. I also recalled those conflicting reports I had received about America from people who had been here or who have relatives in various states and I resolved to do some research and be better enlightened about this country.

The first thing I did was to print the map of America as it is today so that I can see the location and relative size of states.

The most popular states for Kenyans are Texas, Georgia, Kansas, Missouri, Indiana, Iowa, Maryland, Massachusetts, Ohio and California. Others are New York, Washington, New Jersey, Florida and Virginia. Except for California, most of these states are to the south, east and north east. I also noticed that these states have high population of African Americans. Is it a question of like with like? I did not think so because I did not hear Mississippi or Louisiana mentioned and yet I understand these are predominantly black states. I thought I should stop there and leave that research for another time.

Comparing Kenya and Texas was amazing. Texas as a state is bigger than Kenya as a country. Texas is 268,581 sq. miles and Kenya is 224, 961 sq. miles. In terms of population, Kenya is currently estimated at 36 million as compared to Texas 21 million. I did not think it was worthwhile comparing Texas and Kenya beyond the surface area and population. My feeling was that if Kenya had been as well managed as Texas, I would not have left the country for America. I decided to take my imagination beyond Kenya and compare the fifty sates of USA under one President and the fifty sovereign states

33

of Africa governed by fifty Presidents. How come we do not have even one country offering "green cards" or equivalent program for other Africans to go to live, work and study there? Again I decided I would not be able to get very far trying to get answers to these questions at this time. The best thing will be to go to College and study the history of Africa, America and the rest of the world and I will be able to answer most of these questions.

More help from my host
During the weekends that I did not sign for overtime at Sarah's, I went to stay with Joakim. I shared with him the discussion I was having with Sarah about Texas, USA, Kenya and Africa. I learnt a lot about Africa from Joakim because he has visited most of the countries when he was working for an African Region non-profit organization. He has also been to some countries in Europe, Asia and Latin America. He has very high regard for America as a model of democracy to the rest of the word. With regard to what makes America a great nation, Joakim says it is the rule of law, freedoms, patriotism and the love of hard work by both rich, middle class and everyone else. He said while in Kenya most of the people live from day to day, Americans start saving for retirement from an early age.

Joakim gave me a copy of a booklet published by American Government Department of Homeland Security entitled: Welcome to the United States: A Guide for New Immigrants. This was the greatest gift to me as a new immigrant. Many questions about how America was founded, how it is governed and especially the step by step process of settling to this country as a new immigrant are answered. There is also a section on rights and privileges first as Permanent Resident and later as Citizen. Reasons to consider becoming a U.S. citizen and the process are explained.

Learning continues
My stay at Sarah's turned out to be more than a job to me. It was a learning experience. After reading the Guide and researching on the Internet, I was able to engage Sarah better with challenging questions about the American way of living.

The first question she asked me every morning before breakfast was how the weather of the day was going to be. I got into the habit of watching the weather channel and checking the internet as my first assignment of the day so as to answer her question. When I asked her why she was so obsessed about the weather, she said that was American and if I was going to live in America I was going to get into that habit too. It did not take long for me to experience what she was talking about. The temperatures were dropping every day and one day in early January, we got up to find the fields and houses covered in snow. It was my turn to ask Sarah what was going on with the weather. The previous day was sunny and hot and suddenly the snow. After breakfast she sat me down at the table and she gave me a lesson about the weather in America. This is how she started:

"Margaret, did you bring winter clothing with you from Kenya?" She asked. I replied I had and she asked to see them. I showed her the clothes I used to wear in Kenya around June, July and August when the weather turned nasty. She laughed and said that was a joke. She picked up her phone and called her daughter and asked her to find time to take me to a store to buy winter clothing because I did not have some.

The next thing Sarah said is an important statement that I will always remember. She said "In America weather and life are intertwined. You must dress for the weather. If you do not pay attention to the weather forecasts your life may be in danger in no time"

After this, Sarah did not need to remind me to check on the weather channel. I did this every morning and every night before going to bed. She told me to pay particular attention to hurricanes and tornadoes. See information Section Appendix II.

Sarah was also interested in investments.
Monday through Friday, she wanted me to tell her the Dow Jones Industrial Average as reported from the New York Stock Exchange. "How many points is the Dow Jones up" she would ask in course

of the day. As a matter of fact, that thing was just a monster to me. I read the figures as reported on TV and told her if it was up or down and by how many points. She told me she and her husband, before he died, were investors and he used to do day trading. "He used to follow very closely Dow Jones and S&P stock indexes before making his investment decisions." She said. What I know now is that Dow Jones and/or S&P 500 have the same meaning as Share Index which I had heard a lot about on Kenyan television. I believe this will make sense after I take economics class in College.

Workplace transition
It was almost two months to the day that I started work at Sarah's house when Joakim told me I should be ready to start my course as CNA at a nearby Nursing Home. At the end of January 2006, I had to give two weeks notice to the agency because the CNA class was to start on Monday 13th February. It was free provided I signed a contact to work for the facility for six months after the training. I would be paid $6.25 per hour for two weeks while in training and this would increase to $7.25 after passing the class test. One month on the floor and then there was going to be a State test. Those who pass the State test would get a $2. = increment from the date they pass to make their pay $9.25 per hour.

I was now so used to sharing an apartment with Joakim that he had become like my second dad. He had shown me how to send money home, where to buy calling cards to keep in touch with family and he had helped me to open a bank account. He worked at the same organization as I was going to train and work for several years as a Medication Aide. His two bed roomed apartment was very close to work and he allowed me to stay in one of the bedrooms until I was ready to rent my own apartment. He was also going to give me a ride during training and thereafter I would sign on the same schedule, 2pm to 10.00pm, for convenience of transportation. I could not ask for more but I did. He had to show me how to drive because I would soon need my own car. This too he agreed to do.

Sorrowful departure from my first employer in U.S.

On January 30, 2006, I gave two weeks notice to quit my job. When I told Sarah I was leaving she could not believe it because we had bonded like were family. I also felt bad to leave but I had to think about my future. She asked me if she could have her family bypass the agency to hire me direct and pay me more money so that I could stay but I told her money was not the main issue. It was personal development. I was going for training as CNA and hopefully I could apply for the same job later if they needed someone. She asked me to keep in touch.

On February 9, 2006 the agency sent a new hire for me to train. Two days and it was over. On the evening of February 12, 2006 I left Sarah's house. It was parting tears for both of us but I had to leave. I will always cherish the memories.

I had worked for the agency for 12 weeks and made $4,000. = after taxes. Since I was still using the pocket money I brought from home to meet my personal needs I sent all this money to my parents to pay off Nancy's debt. The agreement was to pay back in 24 months but I was going to do it within six months. How about that? This is only possible in America.

My training as a CNA

We started 30 in the class. There were 18 Mexicans, 6 Americans and 6 Africans. Some of the blacks were African Americans but I could not tell the difference. I had read the Welcome Guide for New immigrants and Joakim had also told me in this country you do not ask questions about race, gender, marital status or sex orientation unless someone volunteers the information. There were only three men in the group and the others were girls and middle aged women.

The first thing that impressed me about the class is that although it was starting at 6.00am everyone was on time. People here are very serious about what they have planned to do. Secondly almost everyone was driving a car and had a cell phone. When we got into the class all cell phones were turned off long before the Trainer gave the instructions as a reminder. It appears everyone knew what was expected of them and they did it before it was asked of them. We took 15 minutes break at 8.00am and 45 minutes lunch at 10.00am. The class ended promptly at 2.00pm as scheduled. It was going to be the same routine every day for two weeks when doing theory. The third week we were going to work on the floor. There was going to be a final internal test at the end of that week.

Training was intensive. We had a training guide that the tutor followed supplemented with videos and talks from the department heads about nursing, dietary, housekeeping and administration of the facility. There were tests every morning about what we covered the previous day, a comprehensive weekly test at the end of first and second weeks and final test at the end of third week. During the third week, we were asked to select preferred schedule giving the first and second option. I selected 2 -10pm as first option and the same as second option because I had to have that schedule due to transport. The Director of Nursing called me to explain my choice and she understood I had to have the 2-10pm. As it turned out, the competitive schedule was 6-2 and some with that request had to be moved to 2-10 or 10-6. I learnt later that most of the girls and women had children who had to be taken to school or to a baby sitter in the morning. This is the only way they could come to work because if you leave children unattended they will not only be taken away but you will go to jail.

Everything seemed to be going on very well but every week a few people quit the class for unknown reasons. At the end of the second week, we were about twenty and on the final week there were 15 of us who did the final internal test and signed to start work. This was very surprising to me. Just as the trainees started with enthusiasm so was their determination to quit when they decided to. The lesson I learnt here was that in America people are not coerced to do anything. They do what they will. However, what they decide to do they do well and what they decide to leave they leave as well.

Working and planning for self sufficiency.
The work was demanding but emerging from such thorough training it was not a problem for me. There were many openings for overtime and I could have worked 24 hours if it was humanly possible. Joakim agreed to drop me at work in the morning to do the morning shift and combine with 2-10 or to stay over after 10.00pm to do the 10-6 and pick me up in the morning. By end of June I completed paying the loan advanced by Joyce. She was very happy that we kept our promise. Come July and I would have bought a car and moved to my own apartment but I was in no hurry. Joakim's daughter came to visit him from Canada in August and we had a very good time. In preparation for life alone, Joakim taught me how to drive and I got my driving license in September 2006. We started looking for an apartment and a car. I signed up for an apartment at a complex next to where we lived and I was going to move in on 1st January. As for the car, he said we should wait until the last week of December 2006 when dealers have genuine sales to improve quotas for the year. Just as Joakim predicted I bought a 2003 Toyota Corolla with 29,000 miles for $10,999.- a mark down of $4,000.= from original price of $14,999.= We had offered $12,500 for the same car at the same dealership two weeks earlier and they would not take it. Planning, timing and waiting paid dividends.

Living the American Dream
One year after arriving in America with only high school diploma in my hands and no working experience anywhere, I was renting my own apartment for $800.= per month, driving an almost new Toyota Corolla, which is now loan free, and making plans to go to College in the fall to take preliminary classes for Registered Nurse Course which I should be joining next year. I have kept my job with the same employer and I have no intention of changing because I am very happy there. I miss the physical presence of my parents and siblings but we keep in touch through calling cards.

The purpose of telling this story is not to brag about my achievements or make it seem easy. I want everyone out there to know that with faith, determination and hard work everything is possible. However, the conditions have to be right for one to get the desired results. If I had stayed in Kenya, I believe I would have been successful in Kenyan standards given limitations of job availability and scarce resources. For example getting a job by itself, however low paying, counts as success. However, taking the step to apply for green card was extremely bold given my youth and inexperience but I decided to do it anyway. This step alone put me decades ahead of my peers in Kenya and also put me in a position where I can go for higher education while I work, help my parents and siblings in a way I would never have done before and hopefully bring one or two to live with me in America.

I attribute my success to date first to my parents who brought me up in a disciplined and Godly manner. Dad has confidence in me and he always has words of encouragement such as his 'dream'. Secondly meeting Lisa, who was fifteen years my senior helped me to "think outside the box" by exposing me to knowledge about green card and last but not the least to Joakim, who embraced me like his own daughter and took me step by step in the settling process in USA until I was able to live on my own. I especially recall his words on the day he was driving me to enroll for the CNA course. He said, "This two week course is small investment that brings great returns. As long as you protect your license, you will have more work than you can handle. It is also an appropriate prerequisite for other healthcare courses like Medication Aide, LVN and RN". How right he was! Whenever I talk to my sisters I tell them how tired I am and they wish they were here to get tired but reap the benefits of gainful employment. I have since met Kenyans who came here before me and enrolled in courses that take years to complete and when they encounter financial or logistical difficulties they come back to CNA.

My parents are very anxious to meet Joakim and tell him "thank you" in person. There are very few people who would be so gracious. Joakim and I have maintained a hotline. If I need anything I can call him any time and he can do the same. Even though my parents are very far, with Joakim I feel I have family around. Thank you Lisa, thank you Joakim!

VISA

Understanding types of visas, their rights and privileges is important to visitors, students, aspiring and new immigrants so as to remain in status while in the USA.
For more and latest information please go to http://www. unitedstatesvisas.gov/ .

Whenever I talked about green card, I understood it to mean 'special permission' to travel and live in America which of course it is. I was, however, getting confused when green card was also called a visa. My understanding of visa was in relation to visitors, students and business people. They come to America for a limited time and for specified reason. When I got to know green card is also a type of visa and that it is available in ways other than lottery I decided to do research and get the real meaning of a visa.

What is a visa?

There are two main types. We have **Immigrant visa** and **Nonimmigrant visa**.
An immigrant visa is a document issued by a U.S. consular officer abroad that allows you to travel to the United States and apply for admission as a legal permanent resident (LPR). An immigration inspector of U.S. Customs and Border Protection of the Department of Homeland Security makes the final decision as to whether or not to admit you as an LPR. Once you are admitted as an LPR, you generally have the right to live and work in the United States permanently. U.S. Citizenship and Immigration Services of the Department of Homeland Security will mail your permanent resident card (often called a "green card") to your new address in the United States, usually within three months of your entry into the United States.

A nonimmigrant visa is generally for short-term visitors to the United States. You cannot stay in the United States permanently on a nonimmigrant visa, and you generally cannot work. A nonimmigrant visa is sometimes informally called a "tourist visa" but can be issued for reasons other than tourism, such as medical treatment, business or study. When you enter the United States, you will be given a small card called an I-94 card. The Customs and Border Protection officer will stamp the card with a date as you enter the country. That is the date by which you must leave, even if you still have a valid visa stamped in your passport when that date arrives. However, if your visa is "multiple entries," you can use it to reenter the United States as soon as you like. Most visitor visas permit multiple entries, but some visas only allow one visit and you cannot return with the same visa.

Does a visa guarantee me entry into the United States?

The visa is issued by the Department of State Consular Office abroad, a separate United States agency. The U.S. Citizenship and Immigration Services (USCIS)-has the authority to deny admission at the port of entry. The USCIS also determines how long you remain in the United States; the Department of State Consular Office does not make this determination, even though it issues the visa. Though rare, people who have valid visas are known to have been turned right back at the ports of entry if there are issues that warrant rejecting them to enter the United States.

What if I wish to stay after my I-94 card date requires me to leave

In order to stay beyond the time limit set on your I-94 card, you will need to file Form I-539, Application to Extend Status with the USCIS. The decision to grant or deny the request is solely in the hands of the USCIS. Be sure to allow adequate time for the USCIS to review your application for an extension.

Who are illegal immigrants?

These are humans with body and soul but 'no voice'. They are therefore said to live under the shadows because according to the law they should be apprehended and deported to their home countries. One becomes illegal in one of two ways:

a) Crossing the boarder illegally

b) Overstaying or violating ones visa

It is estimated that there are between 8 and 20 million illegal immigrants in USA. Majority are from Latin America and especially Mexico. Illegal border crossings account for about 60% while visa overstays is 40%. Most illegal immigrants from outside Latin America are visa overstays because there is no border to cross.

The 'no voice' aspect is significant because an illegal immigrant can suffer abuse silently afraid to draw attention to themselves for fear of deportation.

Illegal immigration is a thorny issue in American politics. It has been the subject of great political debates and the media since I have been here. The most remarkable was the Bipartisan Comprehensive Immigration Review Bill that had very strong support of the President and His Administration but still could not see the light of day in the Senate on June 28, 2007. This was great disappointment to the President and other supporters but a great demonstration of the balance of power in American politics.

Immigrant Student Adjustment and Access to Higher Education / DREAM Act formed a part of the comprehensive legislation. It was later reintroduced separately but to no avail. A bipartisan vote of 54-44 in the Senate on 24th October 2007 voted in favor of debate but failed to muster the necessary 60 votes to overcome cloture. A major development between the comprehensive bill and the Dream Act was that the White House actually opposed the latter. Consequently, like the comprehensive legislation that went before, it is resting in peace.

David Jarman wrote:

There seemed to be something for everyone to hate in the latest stab at comprehensive immigration reform. Immigrant groups thought it offered little hope to low-skilled, mostly Hispanic, would-be migrants and jeopardized re-unification of family members.

Right-wingers contended that it was nothing but "amnesty" for illegals. Companies said it imposed excessive bureaucratic burdens on employers. Left-wingers complained that it would depress low-end wages of American workers.

Let's look at the facts. Each year approximately 1.5 million foreigners enter this country, the overwhelming majority in search of work. Unlike the early 20th century when the majority of newcomers were from Europe, today more than half come from Latin America and a quarter from Asia. The problem is that the U.S. immigration system accommodates only about 1 million; the remaining 500 thousand are illegals, undermining the rule of law, endangering U.S. security and souring native-born Americans' attitudes on all newcomers.

Should these trends continue, America's ethnic profile in 2050 will look much different: Hispanics will grow from 12 percent to 25 percent of the total and Asians from 4 percent to 8 percent, while non-Hispanic whites will shrink from 69 percent to 50 percent and blacks will remain unchanged at 14 percent. This changed ethnic profile could significantly reshape our politics and culture.

Immigration is essential to the functioning of the American economy in today's age of globalization. Immigrants, both legal and illegal, provide a means to match the gap between supply and demand for workers, both skilled and unskilled. Highly skilled immigrants, perhaps 15 percent of the current annual influx, make up some 25 percent of our doctors, nurses and PhDs and 40 percent of our top scientists and engineers.

Unskilled labor is particularly scarce in America, as the share of native-born workers with less than a high-school diploma has fallen from 50 percent in 1960 to 12 percent today. The gap is filled by immigrant workers; some 24 percent of farm workers, 17 percent of cleaners and 14 percent of construction workers are illegal immigrants. Immigrants, both legal and illegal, benefit the businesses that hire them and benefit consumers by providing lower-priced goods and services.

The fiscal burden of illegal immigrants is mixed. The cost of providing K-12 education and emergency medical care is borne at the state and local level and may exceed the gains from sales-tax revenue and needed labor. However, at the federal level the benefits clearly exceed the costs, as illegals contribute each year to Social Security and receive no corresponding benefits. Social Security actuaries calculate that over the next 75 years all immigrants (legal and illegal) will pay some $5 trillion more in payroll taxes than they receive in benefits.

The effects of not reaching a viable compromise are serious. First, illegal immigration will continue to grow. Second, improvements to border security will not occur; the current system will continue to be laughably inadequate. Third, local and state governments will take steps to address their individual situations, often in ways that will be disruptive and unhelpful. Fourth, the gap between supply and demand for workers will grow, and economic growth and price stability will be hampered. Tamar Jacoby, senior fellow at the Manhattan Institute, says the important question is how to structure a system going forward that grapples with globalization and the choices it poses for America. This means a flexible system that strikes the right balance between skilled and unskilled, and between temporary and permanent. This will likely result in more permanent immigrant workers, and a flexible mix of skilled and unskilled, depending on economic conditions.

If we establish a flexible program to address future immigration, the status of past illegals becomes less important. In fact, it may prove that the Senate bill approved in 2006, establishing a legal path only for those illegals with over five years residence in-country, may prove a possible compromise. All sides should recognize that it is in their joint interests to reach closure.

David Jarman is a Resident of City County and he gave authority to reproduce this piece.

WEATHER

For more and latest information go to:
http://www.ready.gov/ and http://www.nws.noaa.gov/

Hurricanes

Hurricanes are severe tropical storms that form in the southern Atlantic Ocean, Caribbean Sea, Gulf of Mexico, and in the eastern Pacific Ocean. Scientists can now predict hurricanes, but people who live in coastal communities should plan what they will do if they are told to evacuate.

Prepare for Hurricanes

Get a kit of emergency supplies and prepare a portable kit in case you have to evacuate.

Familiarize yourself with the terms that are used to identify a hurricane.

A **hurricane watch** means a hurricane is possible in your area. Be prepared to evacuate. Monitor local radio and television news outlets or listen to NOAA Weather Radio for the latest developments.

A **hurricane warning** is when a hurricane is expected in your area. If local authorities advise you to evacuate, leave immediately.
- Prepare to secure your property.
- Cover all of your home's windows with pre-cut ply wood or hurricane shutters to protect your windows from high winds.
- Plan to bring in all outdoor furniture, decorations, garbage cans and anything else that is not tied down.
- Keep all trees and shrubs well trimmed.
- If you have a car, fill the gas tank in case you have to evacuate.

Plan to Evacuate

- Plan how you will leave and where you will go if you are advised to evacuate.
- If you do not have a car, plan alternate means of evacuating.
- Plan places where your family will meet, both within and outside of your immediate neighborhood.
- Identify several places you could go in an emergency, a friend's home in another town, a motel or public shelter.
- If you have a car, keep a half tank of gas in it at all times in case you need to evacuate.
- Become familiar with alternate routes and other means of transportation out of your area.
- Take your emergency supply kit.
- Lock the door behind you.
- Take your pets with you, but understand that only service animals may be permitted in public shelters. Plan how you will care for your pets in an emergency.

If time allows:

- Call or email the "out-of-state" contact in your family communications plan.
- Tell them where you are going.
- Leave a note telling others when you left and where you are going.
- Check with neighbors who may need a ride.

If you are not able to evacuate, stay indoors away from all windows. Take shelter in an interior room with no windows if possible. Be aware that there may be a sudden lull in the storm as the eye of the hurricane moves over. Stay in your shelter until local authorities say it is safe.

Stay informed

Local authorities may not immediately be able to provide information on what is happening and what you should do. However, you should listen to NOAA Weather Radio, watch TV, listen to the radio or check the Internet often for official news and instructions as they become available.

Stay out of flood waters, if possible.

The water may be contaminated or electrically charged. However, should you find yourself trapped in your vehicle in rising water get out immediately and seek higher ground.

- Be alert for <u>tornadoes</u> and <u>flooding</u>. If you see a funnel cloud or if local authorities issue a tornado warning take shelter underground, if possible or in an interior room away from windows. If waters are rising quickly or local authorities issue a floor of flash flood warning, seek higher ground.
- Stay away from downed power lines to avoid the risk of electric shock or electrocution.
- Do not return to your home until local authorities say it is safe. Even after the hurricane and after flood waters recede, roads may be weakened and could collapse. Buildings may be unstable, and drinking water may be contaminated. Use common sense and exercise caution.

What is a Tornado?

Tornadoes are nature's most violent storms. Tornadoes must always be taken seriously. Tornadoes can be very dangerous -- sometimes even deadly. They come from powerful thunderstorms and appear as rotating, funnel-shaped clouds. Tornado winds can reach 300 miles per hour. They cause damage when they touch down on the ground. They can damage an area one mile wide and 50 miles long. Every state is at some risk, but states in "Tornado Alley" have the highest risk. Tornadoes can form any time of the year, but the season runs from March to August. The ability to predict tornadoes is limited. Usually a community will have at least a few minutes warning. The most important thing to do is TAKE SHELTER when a tornado is nearby.

Important Terms to Know:

Tornado Watch -- Tornadoes are possible. Stay tuned to the radio or television news.

Tornado Warning -- A tornado has been sighted. Take shelter immediately

To see complete guide, including images, go to: http://www. uscis.gov/files/nativedocuments/M-618.pdf.

About This Guide

Adjusting to your new life in the United States of America will take time. This guide contains basic information that will help you settle in the United States and find what you and your family need for everyday life. It also summarizes important information about your legal status and about agencies and organizations that provide documents or essential services you may need.

As a permanent resident, you should begin to learn about this country, its people, and its system of government. Use this guide to find out about your rights and responsibilities as a new immigrant, to understand how our federal, state, and local governments work, and to learn how important historical events have shaped the United States. This guide also explains the importance of getting involved in your own community and offers suggestions to help you do so.

This guide provides a general summary of rights, responsibilities, and procedures related to permanent residents. To get more specific and detailed information, you should consult the laws, regulations, forms, and guidance of U.S. Citizenship and Immigration Services (USCIS). You should always consult these more detailed resources for your specific immigration question or case. Most of the information you need can be found on the USCIS website at http://www.uscis. gov. You can obtain USCIS forms by calling 1-800-870-3676 and you can get more information by calling the USCIS National Customer Service Center at 1-800-375-5283 or 1-800-767-1833 (for hearing impaired).

Where to Get Help

This guide will help you get started, but it cannot answer all the questions you have about life in the United States. To find additional information, you may wish to contact a state, county, or city government office to learn about services you need or consult with a local organization that helps new immigrants settle into life here. You can find these offices and organizations by using the free resources described below.

The Public Library

Public libraries in the United States are free and open to everyone. Libraries are located in almost every community. The library staff can help you find information on almost any topic and can give you a library card that allows you to borrow items, such as books and videotapes, free of charge. Most libraries also have local newspapers for you to read and computers that you can use to search the Internet. Ask the library staff to show you how to use the computer to search the Internet.

Some libraries give free classes on how to search the Internet. Some libraries also provide English language tutoring or classes and other programs for children and adults.

Your Local Phone Book

Your local "phone book" (telephone directory) contains phone numbers and important information about federal, state, and local community services. The phone book has emergency information, local maps, and information about how to get phone service. The white pages list phone numbers of individual people; the yellow pages have phone numbers and addresses for businesses and organizations; and the blue pages show local, state, and federal government office phone numbers and addresses. You can also dial 411 on your phone to get a specific phone number anywhere in the United States. Your community or city also may have a separate book with the yellow pages listings or its own community phone book.

The Internet
The Internet can link you to many sources of information, including the websites of federal, state, and local government agencies. Most government websites end with ".gov". If you don't have a computer at home, you can use one in your public library or at an "Internet café," which is a business that charges a fee for using a computer with Internet service. You can use the Internet to search for jobs, find housing, learn about schools for your children, and locate community organizations and resources to help you. You also can discover interesting information on the Internet about life in America, United States history and government, and your local community.

• TIP: As an immigrant you should be aware that dishonest people have made websites that look like government websites to confuse you and take advantage of you. Remember that http://www.uscis.gov is the official website of U.S. Citizenship and Immigration Services.

Community-and Faith-Based Organizations That Assist Immigrants
There are organizations in many communities that provide free or very low-cost assistance to immigrants. These organizations can help you learn about your community and the services available to you as an immigrant. You can look for these organizations by searching on the Internet, looking in your local phone book, asking at the public library, and asking your local government social service agency.

Getting Involved in Your Community
Getting involved in your community will help you feel at home here. Your community is also a good source of information. Here are some ways to get involved:
- Introduce yourself to and get to know your neighbors.
- Talk with or visit community organizations that help immigrants get settled in the U.S.
- Join groups at your place of worship.
- Join your neighborhood association. This is a group of people in the neighborhood who meet to work together on things affecting the neighborhood.

- Volunteer at a community organization, school, or place of worship.
- Enroll in an English language class.

You can find more ideas about getting involved on the Department of Housing and Urban Development's web-site at http://www.hud. gov. Look in the "Communities" section for information about communities and suggestions for getting involved.

TO GET MORE INFORMATION FROM USCIS:
.Visit our website at http://www.uscis.gov.
Call our National Customer Service Center:
1-800-375-5283 or 1-800-767-1833 (hearing impaired).
To get USCIS forms, call 1-800-870-3676
or look on the USCIS website.

Getting Settled in the United States

This section provides information that can help you adjust to life in the United States. You'll learn about finding housing and a job, getting a Social Security number and a driver's license, taking care of your money, and getting healthcare for you and your family.

Finding a Place to Live

You can choose where you want to live in the United States. Many people stay with friends or family members when they first arrive. After they find jobs, they move into their own housing. Sometimes religious or community organizations also help with temporary housing.

In the United States, most people spend about 25 percent of their income on housing. Here are some of your housing choices:

Renting a Home
Apartments and houses can be rented. You can find these in several ways:

- Look for "Apartment Available" or "For Rent" signs on buildings.

- Look in the newspaper in the section called "Classified Advertisements" or "Classifieds." Find the pages listing "Apartments for Rent" and "Homes for Rent." These will have information about homes, such as where they are located, the number of rooms, and the cost of rent.

- Look in the phone book yellow pages under "Property Management." These are companies that rent homes. These companies may charge you a fee to help you find a home.

- Ask friends and relatives or people at your job if they know of places to rent.

- Check bulletin boards in libraries, grocery stores, and community centers for "For Rent" notices.

- Check for rentals on the Internet. If you don't have a computer at home, you can go to your local public library or an Internet café.

- Call a local real estate agent.

What to Expect When You Rent a Home

Applying to Rent. People who rent out apartments or homes are called "landlords." A landlord may ask you to fill out a rental application form. This is so the landlord can check to see if you have the money to pay the rent.

The application form may ask for a Social Security number and proof that you are working. You can use your Permanent Resident Card if you do not yet have a Social Security number. You can also show a pay stub from your job to prove you are working. You may also be asked to pay a small application fee.

If you are not yet working, you may need someone to sign the rental agreement with you. This person is called a "co-signer." If you cannot pay the rent, the co-signer will have to pay the rent for you.

Signing a Lease. You sign a rental agreement or "lease" if the landlord agrees to rent to you. When you sign a lease, you agree to pay your rent on time and stay for a specific length of time. Most leases are for 1 year. You can also find housing for shorter periods of time, such as 1 month. You may have to pay more money for a short lease than for a longer one.

When you sign a lease, you agree to keep the home clean and in good shape. You may be charged extra if you damage the place you are renting. The lease may also list the number of people who can live in the home.

A lease is a legal document. You must keep up your part of the agreement. Landlords must also do their part. They must keep the property safe and in good condition.

Paying a Security Deposit. Renters usually pay a security deposit when they move in. This deposit is usually equal to one month's rent. You will get this deposit back if the home is clean and in good condition when you move out. If not, the landlord may keep some or all of your deposit to pay for cleaning or repairs.

Inspect the house or apartment before you move in. Tell the landlord about any problems you find. Talk to your landlord before you move out to find out what you need to fix to get all of your security deposit back.

Paying Other Rental Costs. For some houses or apartments, the rent payment includes the cost of utilities (gas, electricity, heat, water, and trash removal). For other rentals, you must pay separately for these expenses. Ask the landlord if utilities are included when you are looking for housing. If they are, make sure this is in your rental agreement before you sign it. If utilities are not included, you should find out how much they will cost. The cost of some utilities will be more in the summer (for air conditioning) or winter (for heat).

GETTING THINGS FIXED

Landlords must keep the home or apartment you rent safe and in good condition. If you have a problem:

- First, talk to your landlord. Tell him or her what is wrong and that you want it fixed.

- Next, write a letter to your landlord telling him or her what is wrong. Keep a copy for yourself.

- Finally, call your local Housing Office. Most city or local governments have people who inspect houses for problems. Ask the inspector to visit and show him or her all the problems.

If your landlord does not fix the problems, you may be able to make a legal charge against him or her.

Ending a Lease. Ending a rental agreement is called "terminating your lease." Your landlord may agree to terminate your lease early if he or she can find someone else to rent your home. If not, you may have to pay monthly rent until the end of the lease, even if you are not living there. You also may lose your security deposit if you leave before the end of the lease. Give your landlord a written notice that you want to move out. Most landlords require notice at least 30 days before you want to leave.

KNOW YOUR RIGHTS: DISCRIMINATION IN HOUSING IS NOT ALLOWED

Landlords cannot refuse to rent to you because of who you are. It is against the law for landlords to reject you because of:

- your race or color.

- the country you came from.

- your religion.

- your sex.

- a physical disability.

- your family status, such as whether or not you are married.

If you feel you have been refused housing for any of these reasons, you can contact the U.S. Department of Housing and Urban

Development (HUD) by phone at 1-800-669-9777. Information is given in English and Spanish.

• **TIP:** If you move, you should tell the U.S. Postal Service so it can forward your mail to your new address. You can change your address online at http://www.usps.com or visit your local post office and request a "Moving Guide." Don't forget to also file Form AR-11 with DHS. See page 12 for instructions.

Buying a Home
For many people owning a home is part of the "American Dream." Owning a home has many benefits and brings many responsibilities.
Real estate agents can help you find a home to buy. Ask friends or co-workers or call a local real estate agency for the name of an agent. Ask for an agent who knows the area where you want to buy your house. You can look in the newspaper "Classifieds" under "Homes for Sale." You can also look for "For Sale" signs in the neighborhoods you like.

Most people need to get a loan to pay for a home; this is called a "mortgage." You can get a mortgage from a local bank or from a mortgage company. Getting a mortgage means you are borrowing money at a specific rate of interest for a specific period of time. Interest you pay on your mortgage can be deducted from your federal income tax.

• **TIP:** Beware of lenders charging very high interest rates on mortgages. Some lenders may try to charge you more because you are new to this country. There are laws to protect you from fraud, unnecessary expenses, and discrimination in buying a home. Find out more by visiting the "Homes" section at http://www.hud.gov.

You also need to buy homeowner's insurance to help pay for any possible future damage to your home. Insurance usually covers damage due to bad weather, fire, or robbery. You will also need to pay property taxes on the value of your home.

A real estate agent or real estate lawyer can help you find a mortgage and insurance. He or she can also help you fill out the forms to buy your home. A real estate agent should not charge you a fee to buy a home. But you may have to pay a fee to a real estate lawyer to help you fill out the forms. You will also have to pay fees to get your mortgage and to file legal forms with the state. These fees are called "closing costs." Your real estate agent or mortgage lender must tell you how much these fees will be before you sign the final purchase forms for your home.

MORE INFORMATION ABOUT BUYING OR RENTING A HOME

Visit the U.S. Department of Housing and Urban Development website at http://www.hud.gov or call 1-800-569-4287 for information in English and Spanish. For information about buying a home and getting a mortgage, visit the Federal Citizen Information Center at http://www.pueblo.gsa.gov. See also the "For Homeowners and Home Buyers" section of http://www.fanniemae.com.

Getting a Social Security Number

As a permanent resident, you can get a Social Security number (SSN). A Social Security number is a number assigned to you by the United States government. It helps the government keep track of your earnings and the benefits you can get. It is also used by banks and other agencies, such as schools, to identify you. You may be asked for your SSN when you rent an apartment or buy a home.
The government department in charge of Social Security is called the Social Security Administration.

Find the Social Security office closest to you by:
- Asking friends or neighbors where to find the nearest Social Security office.

- Calling 1-800-772-1213 between 7 AM and 7 PM. Information is given in English and Spanish. Free interpreter services are available.

- Looking for the address in the blue pages of the phone book.

- Looking on the Social Security Administration website at http://www.socialsecurity.gov.

You do not need to fill out an application or go to a Social Security office to get a Social Security number if:

- You asked for a Social Security number or card when you applied for an immigrant visa AND

- You applied for an immigrant visa in October 2002 or later AND

- You were age 18 or older when you came to the United States.

In this situation, the information needed to assign you an SSN was sent by the Departments of State and Homeland Security to the Social Security Administration. The Social Security Administration will assign you an SSN and mail your SSN card to the same U.S. mailing address where USCIS sends your Permanent Resident Card. You should get your SSN card within 3 weeks after you arrive in the U.S Contact the Social Security Administration if you do not get your card within 3 weeks after coming to the U.S. or if you change your mailing address after you come to the U.S. but before you receive your SSN card.

You <u>must</u> go to a Social Security office to get an SSN if:

- You did not ask for a Social Security number or card when you applied for an immigrant visa OR

- You applied for your immigrant visa before October 2002 OR

- You were under age 18 when you came to the U.S.

A Social Security representative will help you apply for an SSN. Bring these documents with you when you go to the office to apply:

- A birth certificate or other document such as your passport showing when and where you were born AND

- A document showing your immigration status, including your permission to work in the U.S. This can be your Permanent Resident Card or passport with an immigration stamp or visa label.

Your Social Security number will be sent to you in the mail. You should get your Social Security card about 2 weeks after the Social Security Administration has all documents needed for your application. If they need to verify any of your documents, it may take longer to get your SSN.

IF YOU DO NOT SPEAK ENGLISH

The Social Security office can provide an interpreter free of charge to help you apply for a Social Security number. Tell the person who answers the phone at 1-800-772-1213 that you don't speak English. They will find an interpreter to help on the phone. You can also get help from an interpreter when you visit the Social Security office.

The Social Security Administration website contains helpful information for people new to the United States. A section of the website has information about Social Security in 14 languages. Visit http://www.socialsecurity.gov.

AVOID IDENTITY THEFT

"Identity theft" means someone has stolen your personal information, such as your Social Security or bank account number. They can use it to take money from your bank account or get a credit card in your name. Identity theft is a serious crime. Protect yourself by:

- Making sure you know and trust the people or businesses you give your personal information to, especially on the phone or Internet.

- Leaving your Social Security card at home in a safe place. Do not carry it with you.

- Carrying with you only the identification documents or credit cards you need at the time. Leave the rest at home in a safe place.

- Tearing up or shredding any paper or forms with your personal information on them before throwing them in the trash.

If you have a problem with identity theft, you can get help by calling the Federal Trade Commission's ID Theft Hotline at 1-877-438-4338. You also can get information at http://www.consumer.gov/idtheft.

Taking Care of Your Money

Getting a Bank Account
A bank account is a safe place to keep your money. Banks have different kinds of accounts. Checking accounts (for paying bills) and savings accounts (for earning interest on your money) are two common ones. You can open an account for yourself or a joint account with your spouse or another person. Banks may charge you fees for some of their services.

Credit unions and savings and loan associations are other choices for banking. Your employer may have a credit union that you can join. Credit unions provide most of the same services as banks, but many offer extra services. Compare the services, fees, hours, and locations of banks before you open an account, so you can choose one that best meets your needs.

• **TIP:** Many stores offer check-cashing services and overseas money-wiring services, but these cost money. Check to see if your bank offers these services at a lower cost.

When you open a bank account, you will be asked to prove your identity. You can use your Permanent Resident Card or driver's license. You will also need to give the bank some money—called a "deposit"—to put into your new account. After a few days, you can take money out of your account. This is called "withdrawing" money. You can withdraw money by writing a check, going to an Automatic Teller Machine (ATM), or filling out a withdrawal form in the bank.

Using Your Bank Account
You can get money from your bank account using a personal check or ATM card. Be sure that only you and, if you have one, your joint account holder have access to your account.

Personal checks. You will get a supply of personal checks when you open your checking account. These checks are forms that you fill out to pay for something. Checks tell your bank to pay the person or business you have written on the check. Keep these checks in a safe place.

ATM cards. You can ask your bank for an ATM card. This is a small plastic card linked to your bank account. Use this card to get cash or deposit money in your account at an ATM machine. Usually you do not pay a fee for using your own bank's ATM. You may pay a fee if you use an ATM at another bank.

The bank staff will show you how to use an ATM card and give you a special number, called a PIN ("personal identification number") to use at the ATM. Be careful when using ATMs. Never give anyone your PIN number or ATM card. They could use it to take money out of your account.

Debit cards. Your bank may give you a debit card to use for your checking account. Sometimes your ATM card can also be used as a debit card. Debit cards allow you

to pay for something without writing a check by having your bank send the money directly to the business you are buying from.

Bank checks. Bank checks are checks that the bank makes out at your request. You give the bank money and they make out a bank check for that amount of money to the person or business you want to send it to. Banks may charge a fee for bank checks.

KEEPING YOUR MONEY SAFE

It is not safe to leave large amounts of money in your house. It is also not safe to carry around large amounts of cash. It could be stolen or lost. Your money is protected if you put it in a bank that is a member of the Federal Deposit Insurance Corporation (FDIC). The FDIC provides banks with insurance to protect your money. If your bank closes, the FDIC will pay you the amount of the money in your account up to $100,000. Make sure the bank you choose has FDIC insurance.

CREDIT CARDS

Credit cards—also called "charge cards"—allow you to make purchases and pay for them later. Banks, stores, and gas stations are some businesses that can give you a credit card. You get a bill in the mail each month for purchases you have made with your credit card.

If you pay the entire amount on the bill when you get it, you do not have to pay interest. If you do not pay the entire amount or if you send your payment late, you will be charged interest and possibly an additional fee. Some credit cards have very high interest rates.

Be careful about giving your credit card number to others, especially over the phone or on the Internet. Be sure you know and trust the person or business that asks for your number.

• **TIP:** Check your credit card bill each month to make sure all the charges are correct. If you see a charge that you did not make, call the credit card company immediately. You usually do not have to pay for charges you did not make if you tell the credit card company right away.

Write down the numbers for all bank accounts and debit, ATM, and credit cards. Also write down the phone numbers of these companies. Keep this information in a safe place. If your wallet is lost or stolen, you can call the companies and cancel all your cards. This will keep someone else from using your cards illegally.

YOUR CREDIT RATING

In the U.S., the way you handle your credit is very important. There are organizations that create a "credit score" or "credit rating" for you depending on how you pay bills, how many loans you take out, and other factors. This credit rating is very important when you want to buy a home or car or take out a loan. Here are some things you can do to get a good credit rating:

- Pay all your bills on time.

- Keep your credit card balances low. Pay at least the minimum amount due each month.

- Don't apply for a lot of loans or credit cards.

Under federal law, you can get one free credit report once a year. If you would like to get a copy of your credit rating report, you can call 1-877-322-8228 or go to http://www.annualcreditreport.com. Depending on what state you live in, you may not be able to get the free report until September 1, 2005. This is when people all over the U.S. can get a free credit report.

Looking for a Job

There are many ways to look for a job in the United States. To increase your chances of finding a job, you can:

- Ask friends, neighbors, family, or others in your community about job openings or good places to work.

- Look in the newspaper "Classifieds" section under "Employment."

- Look for "Help Wanted" signs in the windows of local businesses.

- Go to the Employment or Human Resources offices of businesses in your area to ask about job openings.

- Visit community agencies that help immigrants find jobs or job training programs.

- Check bulletin boards in local libraries, grocery stores, and community centers for notices of job openings.

- Check with the department of employment services for your state.

- Search for jobs on the Internet. If you are using a computer at your library, the library staff can help you get started.

Applying for a Job

Most employers will ask you to fill out a job application. This is a form with questions about your address, education, and past work experience. It may also ask for information
about people you have worked with in the past. These are called "references," and the employer may want to call them to ask questions about you.

You may need to create a "resumé" with a list of your work experience. A resumé tells your employer about your past jobs, your education or training, and your job skills. Take your resumé when you apply for work.

A good resumé:

• Has your name, address, and phone number.

• Lists your past jobs and includes dates you worked.

• Shows your level of education.

• Shows any special skills you have.

• Is easy to read and has no mistakes.

Check with local community service agencies to see if they can help you write a resumé. Private businesses can help with this, too, but they charge a fee.

The Job Interview

Employers may want to meet with you to talk about the job. They will ask about your past work and your skills. You can practice answering questions about your past work and your skills with a friend or family member so you will be ready. You can also ask questions of the employer. This is a good chance to find out about the job.

You may want to ask:

- What are the hours of work?

- How much does the job pay? (U.S. law requires most employers to pay a "minimum wage," which is the lowest wage permitted.)

- How many vacation days are there?

- How many sick days are there?

- What benefits come with the job?

During the interview, an employer can ask you many questions. But employers are not allowed to ask some questions. No one should ask you about your race, color, sex, marriage, religion, country of origin, age, or any disability you may have.

WHAT ARE BENEFITS?

In addition to your pay, some employers provide extra employment "benefits." Benefits may include:

- Medical care.

- Dental care.

- Eye care.

- Life insurance.

- Retirement plan.

Employers may pay some or all of the costs of these benefits. Ask about the benefits your employer will provide.

KNOW YOUR RIGHTS: FEDERAL LAWS PROTECT EMPLOYEES

Several federal laws forbid employers from discriminating against people looking for a job. The United States has laws forbidding discrimination because of:

- Race, color, religion, country of origin, and sex (Civil Rights Act).

- Age (Age Discrimination in Employment Act).

- Disabilities (Americans with Disabilities Act).

- Sex (Equal Pay Act).

For more information about these protections, visit the U.S. Equal Employment Opportunity Commission website at http://www.eeoc.gov or call 1-800-669-4000 and 1-800-669-6820 (for hearing impaired).

Other laws help keep work places safe, provide for leave in cases of family or medical emergencies, and provide temporary funds for unemployed workers. Visit the U.S. Department of Labor website at http://www.dol.gov for more information about workers' rights.

What to Expect When You Are Hired

When you go to your new job for the first time, you will be asked to fill out some forms. These include:
- Form I-9, the Employment Eligibility Verification Form. By law, your employer must check to see that all newly hired workers are eligible to work in the U.S. On your first day of work, you will need to fill in the I-9 form. Within 3 business days, you must show your employer your identity documents and work

authorization documents. You can choose what documents to show as proof of your right to work in the U.S., as long as the document is listed on the I-9 form. The list of acceptable documents is on the back of the I-9 form. Examples of acceptable documents are your Permanent Resident Card or an unrestricted Social Security number card in combination with a state-issued driver's license.

- Form W-4, Employee's Withholding Allowance Certificate. Your employer should take federal taxes from your paycheck to send to the government. This is called "withholding tax." Form W-4 tells your employer to withhold taxes and helps you figure out the right amount to withhold.

- Other Forms. You may also need to fill out a tax withholding form for the state you live in and forms so that you can get benefits.

You may be paid each week, every two weeks, or once a month. Your paycheck will show the amount taken out for federal and state taxes, Social Security taxes, and any employment benefits you pay. Some employers will send your pay directly to your bank; this is called "direct deposit."

Speaking English at Work
If you do not speak English, try to learn it as soon as possible. You can find free or low-cost English language classes in your community, often through the local public schools or community college. Knowing English will help you in your job, your community, and your daily life. See page 60 for more information on learning English.

If your employer says you must speak English at work, he or she must show that speaking English is required for you to do your job correctly. Your employer must also tell you that English is required before you are hired. If your employer cannot show that speaking English is required for your job, he or she may be breaking a federal law. If you need assistance or more information, you can contact the U.S. Equal Employment Opportunity Commission (EEOC). Call 1-800-669-4000 or 1-800-669- 6820 (hearing impaired) or go to http://www.eeoc.gov.

FEDERAL PROTECTION FOR IMMIGRANT WORKERS

Federal law says that employers cannot discriminate against you because of your immigration status. Employers cannot:

- Refuse to hire you, or fire you, because of your immigration status or because you are not a U.S. citizen.

- Require you to show a Permanent Resident Card, or reject your lawful work papers.

- Prefer hiring undocumented workers.

- Discriminate against you because of your national origin (or country of origin).

- Retaliate against any employee who complains of the above treatment.

For more information about your rights, or to file a complaint, call the Office of Special Counsel at 1-800-255-7688 or 1-800-237-2515 (for hearing impaired). If you do not speak English, interpreters are available to help you. You also can visit http://www.usdoj.gov/crt/osc for more information.

Drug Tests and Background Checks
For some jobs, you may be required to take a test to make sure you are not using illegal drugs. Some jobs require that you have a background check, an investigation into your past activities and present circumstances.

Paying Taxes

Taxes are money paid by U.S. citizens and residents to federal, state, and local governments. Taxes pay for services provided by the government. There are different types of taxes, such as income tax, sales tax, and property tax.

Income tax. Income tax is paid to federal, most state, and some local governments. "Taxable income" is money that you get from wages, self-employment, tips, and the sale of property. Most people pay income taxes by having money withheld from their paycheck. The amount of income tax you must pay depends on how much you earn. Income tax rates are lower for people who make less money. Anyone who earns income, resides in the United States, and meets certain requirements needs to file a tax return and pay any taxes they owe.

The Internal Revenue Service (IRS) is the federal agency that collects income tax. Taxpayers file a federal "income tax return" Form 1040 with the IRS each year. Your tax return tells the government how much you earned and how much in taxes was taken out of your paycheck. If you had too much taken out of your paycheck, you will get a refund. If you did not have enough taken out of your paycheck, you must send a payment to the IRS.

Social Security and Medicare taxes. These federal taxes are withheld from your paycheck. Social Security provides benefits for certain retired workers and their families; certain disabled workers and their families; and certain family members of deceased workers. Medicare taxes pay for medical services for most people over age 65.In most cases, you must work a total of 10 years (or 40 quarters) over the course of your life to get Social Security retirement benefits and Medicare benefits. You may need fewer than 10 years of work to get disability benefits or for your family to get survivors' benefits based on your earnings.

Sales taxes. Sales taxes are state and local taxes. These taxes are added to the cost of buying certain things. Sales taxes are based on the cost of the item. Sales taxes help pay for services provided by state and local government, such as roads, police, and firemen.

Property taxes. These are state and local taxes on your house and land. In most places, property taxes help support local public schools and other services.

Getting Help With Your Taxes

As a permanent resident, you are required to file a federal income tax return every year. This return covers your earnings for January to December of the past year. You must file your return by April 15. You can get free help with your tax return at an IRS Taxpayer Assistance Center. You don't need to call ahead.

Taxpayer Assistance Centers are located in communities across the United States. To find the Taxpayer Assistance Center where you live, visit http://www.irs.gov/ localcontacts/index.html. To get help by phone, call the IRS at 1-800-829-1040.

YOUR W-2 FORM: WAGE AND TAX STATEMENT

A W-2 is a federal form that lists your earnings and the taxes you paid for the last tax year. A tax year is from January 1 to December 31 of each year. By law, your employer must send you a W-2 form by January 31 each year. You will receive a W-2 form for each job you have. You must send a copy of your W-2 form with your federal income tax return to the IRS. If you live or work in a state that collects income tax, you must send a copy of your W-2 with your state income tax return.

HOW GOVERNMENT WORKS FOR US

Taxes pay for the services the federal government provides to the people of the United States. Some examples of these services are:

- Keeping our country safe and secure.

- Curing and preventing diseases through research.

- Protecting our money in banks by insuring it.

- Educating children and adults.

- Building and maintaining our roads and highways.

- Providing medical services for the poor and elderly.

- Giving emergency help when natural disasters strike, such as hurricanes, floods, or earthquakes.

Traveling in the United States

There are many ways to travel in the United States. Many cities have buses, trains (also called "subways"), trolleys, or streetcars. Anyone can ride these vehicles for a small fee. In some places, you can buy a card good for several trips on subways or buses. You can also pay for each trip separately. Taxicabs, or "taxis," are cars that take you where you want to go for a fee. Taxis are more expensive than other types of public transportation.

Getting a Driver's License
It is against the law to drive without a driver's license. You must apply for and get a driver's license if you want to drive. You get your driver's license from the state where you live.

Check with the state office that issues driver's licenses to find out how to get one. These offices have different names in each state. Some common names are Department of Motor Vehicles, Department of Transportation, Motor Vehicle Administration, or Department of Public Safety. You can find these offices in the blue pages of the phone book or get more information at http://www.firstgov.gov/Topics/Motor Vehicles.html

Some permanent residents already have a driver's license from another country. You may be able to trade this for a license in your state. Check with your state office to see if you can do this.

• TIP: A driver's license is used for identification in the United States. It's a good idea to get one even if you don't own a car.

If you do not know how to drive, you can take driving lessons. Many public school districts have classes in "driver education." You can also look under "Driving Instruction" in the yellow pages of the phone book.

• TIP: Hitchhiking is not common in the United States. In many places, it is illegal. For safety reasons, do not hitchhike and do not give rides to hitchhikers.

SHOULD I BUY A CAR?

Owning a car can be a convenient way to get around. In the U.S., you must also pay for car insurance, registering your vehicle, and licenses. Heavy traffic can make driving difficult in some cities. Think of all the costs and benefits before you decide to buy a car.

10 TIPS FOR DRIVING SAFELY IN THE U.S.

- Drive on the right-hand side of the road.

- Always have your driver's license and insurance card with you.

- Always wear your seat belt.

- Use proper seat belts and car safety seats for children.

- Use your car's signals to show if you are turning left or right.

- Obey all traffic laws and signals.

- Pull over to the side of the road if an emergency vehicle—police car, fire truck, or ambulance— needs to pass you.

- Do not pass a school bus when its red lights are flashing.

- Do not drive if you have been drinking or taking drugs.

- Be very careful when driving in fog, ice, rain, or snow.

TRAVEL INFORMATION

For bus travel:
Greyhound 1-800-229-9424 or http://www.greyhound.com.

For train travel:
Amtrak 1-800-872-7245 or http://www.amtrak.com.

For air travel: There are many airlines in the U.S. Look in your phone book yellow pages under "Airlines."

Taking Care of Your Health

People in the U.S. pay for their own medical care. Medical care is expensive, so many people buy health insurance. You should get health insurance for yourself and your family as soon as possible.

Employers may offer health insurance as a benefit to their employees. Some employers pay all of your monthly health insurance fee, and some pay only part of the fee. This monthly fee is called a "premium." You may need to pay part of the premium. Usually, employers will deduct the employee's part of the premium from their paycheck.

Doctors send their bills to your health insurance company. The health insurance company will pay for some or all of your medical services. Often you must pay a portion of your medical bills. This is sometimes called a "co-payment."

If you do not have health insurance, you may be able to get federal or state healthcare assistance. In general, most states provide some type of assistance to children and pregnant women. Check with the public health department of your state or town.

If you need urgent medical care, you can go to the emergency room of the nearest hospital. Most hospitals are required by federal law to treat patients with a medical emergency even if the person cannot pay.

Federal and State Health Programs

Medicaid is a joint federal/state program for low-income people. Each state has its own Medicaid guidelines. Medicaid pays for medical services, such as visits to the doctor and hospitalization. Permanent residents who entered the U.S. before August 22, 1996 may be able to get Medicaid if they meet certain conditions. Permanent residents who entered the U.S. on or after August 22, 1996 may be able to get Medicaid if they have lived in the U.S. for 5 years or longer and meet certain conditions.

Medicare is a health insurance program for people 65 years of age or older or who have specific disabilities. Medicare pays for services if you are sick or injured, but does not pay for routine care (such as check-ups with your doctor), dental care, or eye care. Medicare allows the use of discount drug cards for people enrolled in Medicare. These cards may help you save money when you buy prescription drugs. If you are eligible for Medicare, you may be able to get one of these discount cards.

Medicare has two parts, Part A and Part B. Part A is free and pays for hospital care and nursing homes certified by Medicare. Part B pays for visits to the doctor, ambulances, tests, and outpatient hospital care. For Part B, you pay a monthly fee.

Permanent residents can get Medicare Part A and Part B if they meet certain conditions. Those who are 65 and older are automatically in Medicare when they start getting Social Security retirement benefits. If you are not 65 but are eligible for other reasons, call the Social Security office near you for information about enrolling. Generally, you must have worked in the U.S. for 10 years (or 40 quarters) over the course of your life to get these Medicare benefits.

State Children's Health Insurance Program (SCHIP)

Your children may be able to get free or low-cost healthcare if you meet certain conditions. Every state has a health insurance program for infants, children, and teenagers. The insurance pays for doctor visits, prescription medicines, hospital care, and other healthcare services. In most states, children 18 and younger without health insurance whose families meet certain income limits are eligible. Children can get free or low-cost healthcare without affecting their parents' immigration status.

FINDING A CLINIC OR OTHER LOW-COST HEALTHCARE

Clinics are medical offices that provide free or low-cost services. Most communities have at least one clinic. Community organizations that work with immigrants may know of a low-cost or free clinic in your area.

The U.S. Department of Health and Human Services also provides basic healthcare to immigrants. They have a website that lists clinics and other healthcare choices. To find a clinic or doctor near you, visit http://ask.hrsa.gov/pc/. Type in your state or zip code to get the information. You can also look in the yellow pages under "Social Services."

MORE INFORMATION ABOUT MEDICAID AND MEDICARE

Contact the Social Security Administration at 1-800-772-1213 or the Centers for Medicare and Medicaid Service website at http://www.cms.hhs.gov.

MORE INFORMATION ABOUT SCHIP

Each state has its own SCHIP rules. You need to find out about the program in your state. For information about SCHIP in your state, call 1-877-543-7669 or visit http://www.insurekidsnow.gov and enter the name of your state.

Other Federal Benefits Programs

You or members of your family may be eligible for other federal benefits, depending on your immigration status, length of time in the U.S., and income.

The Food Stamp Program

Some low-income immigrants and immigrant children may be eligible for food stamp assistance, depending on their immigration status, length of time in the U.S., and income. Food stamps allow you to obtain some foods free at grocery stores. Some states may have their own state-funded food stamp programs with different rules for eligibility. For information on federal food stamp eligibility from the U.S. Food and Nutrition Service in 34 different languages, visit http://www.fns.usda.gov/fsp/outreach/translations.htm.

Services for Survivors of Domestic Violence

Immigrants and their children who are survivors of domestic violence may be eligible for federal benefits and services, such as battered women's shelters or food stamps. For more information on these services from the U.S. Department of Health and Human Services, visit http://www.hhs.gov/ocr/immigration/bifsltr.html.

Temporary Assistance for Needy Families (TANF) Temporary Assistance for Needy Families is a federal program that gives money to states to provide assistance and work opportunities for low-income families. Immigrants may be eligible, depending on their immigration status, length of time in the U.S., and income. Programs differ by state and some states have their own state-funded assistance program. For links and information on TANF, visit http://www.acf.dhhs.gov/programs/ofa/.

Assistance for Disabled Immigrants

Immigrants with disabilities may be eligible for Medicaid, food stamps, and Supplemental Security Income, depending upon their immigration status, length of time in the U.S., and income. For more information on food stamps, see page 47. For information about Supplemental Security Income, see http://www.ssa.gov/notices/ supplemental-securityincome/spotlights/spot-non-citizens.htm.

One-Stop Career Centers

The federal government funds career centers that offer training referrals, career counseling, job listings, and other employment-related services. English as a Second Language (ESL) classes and job skills training are also offered to immigrants, depending on their immigration status and income, at some of these centers. For information on One-Stop Career Centers throughout the U.S., visit http://www.doleta.gov/usworkforce/onestop/onestopmap.cfm.

• **TIP**: You can visit http://www.govbenefits.gov to find out about services that might be available to you.

Education and Childcare

Education can help connect you and your family to your community. This section describes schools in the United States for children, youth and adults and answers questions you may have about them. It also offers suggestions for finding good childcare, if you have young children at home and need to work.

Education

To make sure all children are prepared to succeed, the U.S. provides free public education. This section tells you how to sign your children up for school. You will learn how U.S. schools work and how to help your children learn.

Enrolling Your Child in School

Most public schools in the United States are co-educational. Co-educational means that girls and boys attend classes together. The United States has compulsory school attendance laws. This means that state laws require all children ages 5 to 16 to attend school in most states. Check with your state department of education to find out the required ages for school attendance in your state.

You can send your child to a public or private school. In most states, parents may also teach their children at home. This is called "home schooling." Public schools are free and do not offer religious instruction. What your children learn in public school is set by the state. However, local teachers and parents decide how it is taught. Your federal and state income taxes and your local property taxes pay for these schools.

Students must pay a fee (called "tuition") to attend private schools. Religious groups run many private schools. Some are co-educational.

Some are only for boys or only for girls. Some offer financial help for students who cannot pay the tuition.

Most American children are in school for 12 years. Your children will be placed in a class (called a "grade") based on their age and how much previous education they have. Sometimes a school may give your child a test to decide what grade he or she should be in.

HOW MOST U.S. SCHOOLS ARE ORGANIZED

Elementary or Primary School
Kindergarten and Grades 1 to 5   Children Ages 5 to 10

Junior or Middle School   Grades 6 to 8,
                                                    Youth Ages 11 to 13

Secondary or High School   Grades 9 to 12,
                                            Young Adults Ages 14 to 18

Postsecondary or Higher
Education, Public and Private
Community Colleges,
2-year or 4-year Colleges or
Universities, Trade Schools   All Adults May Attend

One of the first things you should do is enroll your child in school. Some questions that parents often ask about public schools include:

Q: How long is the school year?

A: The school year usually begins in August or September and ends in May or June. In some places, children attend school all year.

Children are in school Monday through Friday. Some schools offer programs before or after regular school hours for children whose parents work. You may be charged a fee for these programs.

Q: Where do I enroll my child?

A: Call or visit your local school district's main office to find out which school your child should attend. Tell the school staff your child's age and the address where you live.

Q: What documents do I need to enroll my child?

A: You need your child's medical records and proof that they have certain immunizations (also called "shots") to protect them from disease. You also may need proof that you live in the same community as the school. If you have lost these documents, ask school staff how to get new documents. To avoid delays, do this before you try to enroll your child.

Q: What if my child does not speak English?

A: The school is responsible for testing and placing your child in the right program. Schools receive state and federal funds for programs and services like English as a Second Language (ESL) and bilingual education. You can call your child's school to ask about testing, placement, and services. Even if your child does not speak English, he or she needs to learn the academic material for his or her grade level. This can happen through ESL or bilingual education.

Q: What if my child is disabled?

A: Students with a physical or mental disability can get a free public education, just like a child who does not have a disability. Your child will be placed in a regular school classroom, if possible. If your child's disability is severe, he or she may be given special education services outside the regular classroom.

Q: My child was not in school before coming to the United States. How long can he or she attend public school for free?

A: Your child can attend school for free until they reach age 21 in most states. If your child has not graduated from high school by then, he or she can enroll in adult education classes to obtain a General Educational Development (GED) certificate instead of a high school diploma. Call your local school district office or your state department of education to find out where GED classes are offered.

Q: How will my child get to school?

A: Children can sometimes walk to school in the United States. If the school is too far away, they will ride a bus. Public schools have buses, which are free. Students are picked up and dropped off at a school-bus stop near your home. To find out if your child can ride the bus, contact your local school system. If you have a car, you can also set up a "car pool" with other parents in your area to share driving your children to school.

Q: What will my child eat at school?

A: Children can take lunch to school or buy it at the school cafeteria. The U.S. government also provides nutritious free or low-cost breakfast and lunch for children who cannot afford to buy food at school. Call or visit your child's school to find out if it participates in the federal School Meals program. Talk with school staff to find out if your children are eligible to participate.

Q: Who pays for books and school activities?

A: Public schools usually provide free books. Students must usually buy their own school supplies, such as paper and pencils. If you cannot pay for these supplies, contact your child's school. Some schools may charge a small fee for supplies or special events, such as school trips. Many schools offer after-school sports and music programs. You may need to pay a fee for your children to participate in some of these programs.

Q: What will my child learn?

A: Each state sets academic standards for schools. These standards state what all students should know and be able to do. Local school districts decide how this information should be taught. Most schools teach English, math, social studies, science, and physical education. Art, music, and foreign languages are sometimes offered.

Q: How is my child's work judged?

A: Teachers assign grades based on the work your child does during the school year. Grades are usually based on homework, tests, attendance, and class behavior. You will receive a "report card" several times a year. This report card tells you how your child is doing in each subject. Schools have different ways of grading students. Some use letter grades, with A or A+ for excellent work and D or F for poor or failing work. Others use number grades. Others summarize your child's performance with words like "excellent," "good," or "needs improvement." Ask school staff how students in your child's school are graded.

Q: How can I talk to my child's teacher?

A: Most schools have regular parent conferences for you to meet with your child's teacher. You can also schedule meetings to talk with teachers or school administrators about how your child is doing in school. If you do not speak English, ask if there is someone at the school who speaks your language and can help interpret.

Q: What if my child misses school?

A: Being in school is very important. Parents must send a written letter to the teacher or call the school to explain why their child was not in school. Let the teacher know in advance if your child will be out of school. Students must usually make up any work they missed.

Q: What if my child gets into trouble?

A: Many schools have a list of rules that students must obey. These are called "codes of conduct." Ask your child's school about its code of conduct. Students who break school rules may be punished by being required to stay after the school day is over. Or they may not be allowed to participate in sports or other school activities. Physical punishment is NOT permitted in most U.S. schools.

Children may be suspended or expelled from school if they behave very badly and break school rules often. Your child will no longer be able to go to school if he or she is expelled. You will need to meet with school staff to find out how to get your child back in school.

Q: Is my child safe in school?

A: Most American public schools are safe places to learn. But some schools—mainly high schools— have problems with violence, street gangs, or drugs and alcohol. Talk to a teacher, school counselor, or administrator if you are worried about your child's safety.

FEDERAL SCHOOL MEALS PROGRAM

Children learn better when they are well fed. To improve learning, the United States government provides healthy low-cost or free meals to more than 26 million children each school day. Participation in the School Breakfast Program and National School Lunch Program is based on family income and size. The Special Milk Program provides milk to children who do not participate in other federal school meals programs. For more information about these programs, visit the U.S. Department of Agriculture website at http://www.fns. usda.gov/cnd/.

WHAT YOU CAN DO

Most public and private schools have a Parent Teacher Association (PTA) or Parent Teacher Organization (PTO). These groups help parents learn about what is going on in their child's school and how to get involved in school events. Anyone can join, even grandparents. The PTA/PTOs also support schools by sponsoring special activities and by providing volunteers to help out in the classroom. You can get involved even if you do not speak much English. Many schools have information specifically for parents with limited English-speaking skills. Call or visit your school office to find out when the PTA/PTO for your child's school meets and how you can join.

Higher Education: Colleges and Universities

Young adults can continue their education in a 2-year community or technical college or a 4-year college or university after high school. These are called "postsecondary institutions" or "institutions of higher education." There are public and private institutions of higher education. Public colleges and universities cost less than private ones, especially for residents of the state where the college or university is located. Young adults can also choose to attend schools to learn specific jobs, such as repairing computers or being a healthcare assistant.

Students in higher education choose a specific subject to study in depth (this subject is called their "major"). Choosing a major helps prepare them for employment or further education in that field.

Degree Type	Type of School	Years of Schooling
Certificate	Community College/ Trade School	6 months to 2 years

Associate's	Community College	2 years
Bachelor's	4-year College or University	4 years
Master's	University	2 years
Doctorate	University	2–8 years
Professional	Specialized School	2–5 years

A college or university education can be expensive. Some schools provide financial help called "scholarships." The U.S. government also provides financial aid for students. Most students take out a loan or apply for financial aid or scholarships to help pay for their schooling.

Federal Financial Aid for College Students

The U.S. government provides financial help to students attending certain institutions of higher education. This aid covers many school expenses, including tuition, fees, books, room and board, supplies, and transportation. Students qualify for this aid by their financial need, not their grades. There are three types of federal aid:

- Grants—money that you don't have to repay.

- Work Study—money that you earn while you are in school.

- Loans—money that you borrow that you must repay later with interest.

For more information on federal financial aid programs, call 1-800-433-3243 or visit the U.S. Department of Education website http://www.studentaid.ed.gov/ students/publications/student guide/index.html. Information is also available in Spanish.

BEWARE OF FINANCIAL AID FRAUD

Be careful when you are searching for information on student financial assistance. Avoid offers that seem too good to be true or that promise you results in exchange for money. Every year, families lose millions of dollars to "scholarship fraud." If you are the victim of fraud, or for free information, call 1-877-382-4357 or 1-866-653-4261 for hearing impaired, or visit the Federal Trade Commission website at http://www.ftc.gov/scholarshipscams.

Adult Education

Learning does not have to end when you become an adult. In the U.S., people are encouraged to become "lifelong learners." If you are 16 years of age or older and have not completed high school, you can enroll in Adult Secondary Education (ASE) classes. These classes prepare you to earn a General Educational Development (GED) certificate.

A GED certificate is an alternative high school diploma. It shows that you have learned high-school-level academic knowledge and skills. To earn a GED, you must take and pass tests in 5 different areas: reading, writing, social studies, science, and mathematics. Most U.S. employers consider a GED credential to be equal to a regular high school diploma. In many areas, GED preparation classes are free or low-cost. Look in the phone book under "Adult Education" or call your local school district office for information.

Many adults take classes to learn more about a subject that interests them or to learn new skills that can help them in their jobs. Many public school systems and local community colleges offer classes in a wide range of subjects for adults. Anyone can enroll in these classes, which generally have low fees. Check with your local school system or community college to find out what classes are available, how much they cost, and how to enroll.

Learning English

There are many places where you can learn how to speak, read, and write in English. Many children and adults enroll in English as a Second Language (ESL) classes. These classes help people who do not know English to learn the language. These classes are also called English for Speakers of Other Languages (ESOL) or English Literacy classes.

Children who do not know English will learn it in school. America's public schools provide help and instruction for all students who need to learn English. Students who need extra help are often called Limited English Proficient (LEP) students.

Students just beginning to learn English may take an ESL class in place of a regular English class. Students with more English language skills may be placed in a regular classroom and given extra help. Some schools also offer after-school programs and tutoring to help students learn English. Your child's school will tell you what kind of help they give students who need to learn English.

Adults who do not understand English can enroll in an ESL class offered in a public adult and community education program or private language school.

Public adult and community education programs are often offered in local communities by school districts and community colleges. These programs may provide ESL classes along with tutoring from local volunteers. These programs are often free, or you may pay a small fee. Classes may meet during day or evening hours. Call your local community college or school district office to find the nearest ESL program. Look in the blue pages of your phone book under the heading "Schools— Public."

Most large cities also have private language schools that offer day or evening ESL classes. The cost for these classes is often based on the number of hours of instruction. Private language classes are generally more expensive than public classes. To find a private language school, look in the yellow pages of your telephone book under the heading "Language Schools."

Some community organizations, libraries, and religious groups also offer free or low-cost ESL classes. Check with your local public library, social service agency, or place of worship. The reference librarian at the local library can also tell you about ESL programs and show you where to find ESL books, tapes, CDs, and computer software at the library.

CALL 211 FOR INFORMATION ON SOCIAL SERVICES

You can now call 211 in many states to get help finding the services you need. Call 211 to find out where you can enroll in ESL classes in your neighborhood. You can also call 211 if you need help finding food, housing, a drug treatment program, or other social services.

Some states and counties do not yet offer 211 services. If you call and get no answer, this 211 service is not yet available in your community.

Childcare

If you work and your children are too young to go to school, you may need to find someone to watch them while you are at work. Sometimes children in school need someone to watch them when school is over, if their parents cannot be at home. If you or other family members are not able to watch your children, you need to find someone to take care of them. Do not leave young children at home alone.

Finding Childcare

93

Choosing someone to care for your children is an important decision. As you make this decision, think about the quality and cost of care. Try to find a caregiver who is close to your home or job.

There are many resources you can use to find a good childcare provider. Ask other parents, friends, and coworkers who cares for their children. Some states have a childcare referral agency that can give you a list of state-licensed childcare programs. Licensed childcare programs meet specific requirements set by the state for the protection of your children. You also can call your local school district office to find places where other children in your neighborhood are cared for.

• **TIP:** If you need help finding good childcare in your area, the U.S. Department of Health and Human Services has a National Child Care Information Center. Call 1-800-616-2242 for information. You can also find information and answers to questions about how to choose a good program for your child at http: //www. childcareaware. org.

TYPES OF CHILDCARE

You have a number of choices when choosing a childcare provider.

In-Home Care. A caregiver comes into your home to watch your children. This type of service can be expensive, because your child gets more individual attention. The quality of care depends on the person you hire.

Family Childcare. Your child is cared for in somebody else's home with a small group of other children. This can be less expensive than other types of childcare. The quality of care depends on the people who watch your child and the number of children they are caring for in their home.

Daycare Centers: Daycare centers are programs located in schools, churches or other faith-based organizations, and other places. Centers usually have several caregivers who watch larger groups of children. Centers must meet state standards and their staff usually have special training and experience.

Head Start Programs: The federal government provides funding for 'Early Head Start" and 'Head Start" programs for low-income families. These programs provide care and educational services to young children to get them ready for school. To learn more about these programs, call the Department of Health and Human Services at 1-866-763-6481 or visit the website http://www.acf.hhs.gov/programs/hsb/.

Some childcare providers will take care of children for a full day or only part of the day, depending on the parents' needs. Cost is also a factor in choosing a caregiver. Check to see if you are eligible for federal or state childcare assistance. Many states offer financial assistance to low-income parents who are working or participating in job training or education programs.

• **TIP:** Make sure the childcare provider or program you are using is licensed or accredited. "Licensed" means that the program meets minimum safety and care standards set by the state. "Accredited" programs meet higher standards than those required for a state license.

How Can You Tell if a Childcare Provider Is Good?

- Think about these basic questions when you visit a childcare program.

- Are the children happy when around the staff?

- Are toys available that are appropriate for the children's ages?

- Were children doing an appropriate activity?

- Did the provider talk to your child while you were there?

- Is the space clean and organized?

- Is there a curriculum or routine for the children?

Be sure to ask for references so that you can talk to other parents about the program.

LEARNING ABOUT
THE UNITED STATES

The United States is a representative democracy, and citizens here play a very important role in governing the country. In this section, you will learn how citizens help shape the U.S. government, how the United States began and developed, and how our government operates.

We the People: The Role of the Citizen in the United States

In the United States, the government gets its power to govern from the people. We have a government of the people, by the people, and for the people. Citizens in the United States shape their government and its policies, so they must learn about important public issues and get involved in their communities. Citizens vote in free elections to choose important government officials, such as the President, Vice President, Senators, and Representatives. All citizens can call their elected officials to express an opinion, ask for information, or get help with specific on, ask for information, or get help with specific issues.

Our government is based on several important values: freedom, opportunity, equality, and justice. Americans share these values, and these values give us a common civic identity.

Government in the United States protects the rights of each person. The United States is made up of people from different backgrounds, cultures, and religions. Our government and laws are organized so that citizens from different backgrounds and with different beliefs all have the same rights. No one can be punished or harmed for having an opinion or belief that is different from that of most other people.

OF, BY, AND FOR THE PEOPLE: WHAT IS DEMOCRACY?

The word "democracy" means "government by the people." Democracy can have different forms in different countries. In the United States, we have what is called "representative democracy." This means that the people choose officials to represent their views and concerns in government.

How the United States Began

The early colonists and settlers who came to the United States were often fleeing unfair treatment, especially religious persecution, in their home countries. They were seeking freedom and new opportunities. Today, many people come to the United States for these same reasons.

Before it became a separate and independent nation, the United States was made up of 13 colonies that were ruled by Great Britain. People living in the colonies had no say in which laws were passed or how they were governed. They especially objected to "taxation without representation." This means that people had to pay taxes, but they had no say in how their government operated.

By 1776, many people felt that this was unfair and that they should govern themselves. Representatives from the colonies issued a Declaration of Independence. This important document declared that the colonies were free and independent and no longer tied to Great Britain. Thomas Jefferson wrote the Declaration of Independence. He later became the third president of the United States.

WHAT YOU CAN DO

As a permanent resident, you have many rights and freedoms. In return, you have some responsibilities. One important responsibility is to get involved in your community. You should also learn about the American way of life and our history and government. You can do this by taking adult education classes and reading the local newspaper.

THE UNITED STATES AND THE ORIGINAL THIRTEEN COLONIES

The thirteen colonies were founded in the following order:

Virginia, Massachusetts, Maryland, Connecticut, Rhode Island, Delaware, New Hampshire, North Carolina, South Carolina, New Jersey, New York, Pennsylvania, and Georgia.

The Declaration of Independence was signed on July 4, 1776. This is the reason that Americans celebrate July 4th every year as Independence Day: it is our nation's birthday.

The United States had to fight for its freedom from Great Britain in the Revolutionary War. General George Washington led the military forces of the American Revolution. He is known as the "Father of Our Country." Later he became the first president of the United States.

After the colonies won the war, they became states. Each state had its own government. The people in these states wanted to create a new form of government to unite the states into a single nation. Today, this central government, our national government, is called "the federal government." The United States now consists of 50 states, the District of Columbia (a special area that is the home of the federal government), the territories of Guam, American Samoa, and the U.S. Virgin Islands, and the commonwealths of the Northern Mariana Islands and Puerto Rico.

"ALL MEN ARE CREATED EQUAL"

Many Americans know these words from the Declaration of Independence by heart:

"We hold these truths to be self-evident, that all men are created equal, that they are endowed by their Creator with certain unalienable Rights, that among these are Life, Liberty and the pursuit of Happiness."

This means that all people are born with the same basic rights. Government does not create these rights, and no government can take these rights away.

Creating "A More Perfect Union"

For several years after the American Revolution, the states tried different ways to join together in a central government, but this government was too weak. So representatives from each of the states gathered in Philadelphia, Pennsylvania in 1787 to develop a new, stronger central government. This meeting was the Constitutional Convention. After much debate, leaders from the states drafted a document describing this new government. This document is the U.S. Constitution, one of the most important documents in American history. The Constitution described how the new government would be organized, how government officials would be chosen, and what rights the new central government would guarantee to citizens.

The members of the Constitutional Convention approved the Constitution on September 17, 1787. Next, all 13 states had to approve it. Some people felt that the Constitution did not do enough to protect the rights of individual people. The states agreed to approve the Constitution if a list of individual rights were added to it. The states approved the Constitution in 1 789. This list of individual rights, called the Bill of Rights, was added to the Constitution in 1791. Changes to the Constitution are called "amendments." The first 10 amendments to the Constitution are called the Bill of Rights.

The United States is a nation governed by laws. Government officials make decisions based on those laws. The Constitution is known as the "supreme law of the land" because every citizen, including all government officials, and every law that is created must uphold the principles of the Constitution. Laws apply equally to everyone. The federal government has limited powers. Powers not given directly to the federal government by the Constitution are held by the states.

"OLD GLORY"—THE UNITED STATES FLAG

The United States flag has changed over our history. Now it has 13 stripes to represent the original 13 American colonies. It has 50 stars, one for each state. The American national anthem was written about the flag and is called "The Star-Spangled Banner." The flag is also called the "Stars and Stripes," and a favorite American song is called "Stars and Stripes Forever."

"WE THE PEOPLE"

"We the People" are the first three words of the U.S. Constitution. The Constitution begins by explaining why it was written and what it was intended to accomplish. This section is called the "preamble." Here is the preamble to the Constitution:

"We the People of the United States, in Order to form a more perfect Union, establish Justice, insure domestic Tranquility, provide for the common defense, promote the general Welfare, and secure the Blessings of Liberty to ourselves and our Posterity, do ordain and establish this Constitution for the United States of America."

The Bill of Rights: The First 10 Amendments

The first changes to the Constitution were made to protect individual citizens and to limit the power of government. The Bill of Rights lists important freedoms that are promised to the American people. In most instances, these rights limit what government can do to individual people. These rights include:

- Freedom of speech. The government cannot tell people what to say or not say. People can say what they want about public issues without fear of punishment.

- Freedom of religion. The government cannot tell people what place of worship to attend. People can choose to worship—or not worship—as they please.

- Freedom of the press. The government cannot decide what is printed in newspapers or heard on radio and TV.

- Freedom to gather in public places. The government cannot stop people from holding lawful public gatherings for many different purposes.

- Freedom to own firearms. The government cannot prevent people from owning guns.

- Freedom to protest government actions and demand change. The government cannot silence or punish people who challenge government actions they don't agree with.

The Bill of Rights also guarantees "due process." Due process is a set of specific legal procedures that must be followed when someone is accused of a crime. Police officers and soldiers cannot stop and search a person without good reason, and they cannot search people's homes without permission from a court. Persons accused of a crime are guaranteed a speedy trial by a jury made up of people like themselves.

They are guaranteed legal representation and can call witnesses to speak for them. Cruel and unusual punishment is also forbidden.

CHANGING THE CONSTITUTION

The U.S. Constitution is called a "living document" because the American people, acting through their state and national representatives, can change it when necessary. These changes are called "amendments." It is a long and difficult process to change the Constitution, so it has been changed only 27 times over the course of our history. Besides the Bill of Rights, some important amendments are the Thirteenth, which forbids slavery, and the Fourteenth, which guarantees all citizens equal protection under the law. The Nineteenth Amendment gives women the right to vote.

How the Federal Government Works

The original 13 colonies had lived under the total power of the British king. In their new central government, Americans wanted to prevent a concentration of power in one government official or one office. The Constitution created three branches for the federal government, so that power would be balanced. The three branches have separate responsibilities. We call this the system of "checks and balances." No single branch of government can become too powerful because it is balanced by the other two branches.

THE FEDERAL GOVERNMENT

The three branches of the federal government are:

The Legislative branch: the U.S. Congress and related offices

The Executive branch: the President, Vice President and departments of the federal government

The Judicial branch: the Supreme Court of the United States and federal courts across the country

The Legislative Branch: Congress

Citizens of the United States vote in free elections to choose people to represent them in the U.S. Congress. Congress has the responsibility of making the laws for our nation. Congress is made up of the House of Representatives and the Senate.

The U.S. House of Representatives

People in each state vote to choose members of the House of Representatives. There are 435 members of the House of Representatives, which is often called "the House." The number of representatives from each state depends on how many people live in that state. States are divided into districts. People living in each district vote for someone to represent their district in the House. Each representative serves for two years, and then people have another chance to vote for them or for a different person to represent them. Representatives can serve in Congress for an unlimited period of time.

There are five additional members in the House. These are the representatives of the District of Columbia and the territories of

Puerto Rico, Guam, American Samoa, and the U.S. Virgin Islands. They may participate in debates, but they cannot participate in the formal votes of the entire House.

The House of Representatives makes laws, but it has some special responsibilities. Only the House of Representatives can:

- Propose laws about taxes.

- Decide if a government official accused of committing a crime against the country should be put on trial in the Senate. This is called "impeachment."

The U.S. Senate

There are 100 Senators in the U.S. Senate. People in each state vote to choose two Senators to represent them in Congress. Senators serve for six years, and then people have another chance to vote for them or for a different person to represent them. Senators can serve in Congress for an unlimited period of time. Senators make laws, but they also have special responsibilities.

Only the Senate can:

- Say "yes" or "no" to any agreements the President makes with other countries or organizations of countries. These are called "treaties."

- Say "yes" or "no" to any person the President chooses for high-level jobs, such as Supreme Court judges or officials to run the federal departments, such as the Department of Education or the Department of Health and Human Services.

- Hold a trial for a government official who commits a crime against the United States.

The Executive Branch: The President

The President is the leader of the executive branch and is responsible for upholding and enforcing the laws of the country. The President has many other responsibilities, too, such as setting national policies, proposing laws to Congress, and choosing high-level officials and members of the Supreme Court. The President also is the leader of the U.S. military and may be called the Commander-in-Chief.

People vote in elections for the President and Vice President every four years. The President can only serve in office for 2 four-year terms. The Vice President becomes President if the President becomes disabled or dies.

The Judicial Branch: The Supreme Court

The Constitution created the Supreme Court, the highest court in the United States. There are nine judges on the Supreme Court. They are called "justices." The President chooses the members of the Supreme Court, and they serve as long as they are able. The Supreme Court can overrule both state and federal laws if they conflict with the Constitution. There are other federal courts, such as the U.S. District Courts and the U.S. Circuit Courts of Appeals.

To learn more about the U.S. Supreme Court, visit http: / /www. supremecourtus.gov.

State and Local Government

In addition to the federal government, each state has its own constitution and its own government. Each state government also has three branches: legislative, executive, and judicial.

The leader of the state executive branch is called the "governor". The people of each state vote in elections to choose their governor and their representatives to the state legislature. The state legislature makes the laws that apply in each state. These laws cannot conflict with the U.S. Constitution, and each state judicial branch upholds the laws of that state.

Each state also has local governments. There are city or county governments or sometimes both. They provide and oversee many services in your local community, such as public schools and libraries, police and fire departments, and water, gas, and electric services. People in local communities usually vote for local government officials, but some local officials are appointed. Local governments have different forms. Some have mayors as their leaders; some have city councils or county councils. Local communities also have school boards, citizens who are elected or appointed to oversee the public schools.

GOVERNMENT OFFICIALS SERVE THE PEOPLE

In the United States, everyone can call their elected Representative and Senators. You can call 202-224-3121 and ask for your Representative's or Senators' offices. You can write to your Representative or Senators to ask questions or give your opinion about legislation and the federal government, or if you have a problem and need help with federal benefits.

To write to your Representative:

The Honorable (add Representative's full name)

U.S. House of Representatives

Washington, DC 20515

To write to your Senator:

The Honorable (add Senator's full name)

United States Senate

Washington, DC 20510

You can visit the websites of Congress to learn about current activities in the House and Senate and about your own Representative and Senators, including their website addresses.

- For the House of Representatives, visit http://www.house.gov/.

- For the Senate, visit http://www.senate.gov/.

WHAT YOU CAN DO

Many local government meetings are open to the public. Many are held at night so that anyone can attend. For example, you can go to a city council meeting or a school board meeting to learn more about what is going on in your community. These meetings and their times and locations are usually listed in the local newspaper. The meetings may be listed on the local government's website. Some local government meetings also are on television on local cable stations.

WHAT YOU CAN DO

Learn about your Representative and Senators and what they are doing to represent you in Congress. You can do this by looking for stories about them in your local newspaper and visiting the websites for Congress. All Senators and Representatives have local offices in their home communities; you can find these listed in the blue pages of the phone book. If you visit Washington, DC, you can take a free tour of the U.S. Capitol, where Congress works.

You can learn about the President by visiting the website for the White House, the President's home. Visit http://www.whitehouse.gov/.

Becoming a U.S. Citizen

Becoming a U.S. Citizen gives permanent residents new rights and privileges. Citizenship also brings with it new responsibilities. This section offers some reasons to consider becoming a U.S. citizen and describes what you need to do to become a citizen.

To become a citizen, you must be willing to swear your loyalty to the United States. You must give up your allegiance to any other country. You must agree to support and defend the U.S. Constitution. When you become a citizen, you accept all of the responsibilities of being an American. In return, you get certain rights and privileges of citizenship.

Why Become a U.S. Citizen?

Permanent residents have most of the rights of U.S. citizens. But there are many important reasons to consider becoming a U.S. citizen. Here are some good reasons:

- Showing your patriotism. Becoming a citizen is a way to demonstrate your commitment to your new country.

- Voting. Only citizens can vote in federal elections.

- Serving on a jury. Only U.S. citizens can serve on a jury. Serving on a jury is an important responsibility for U.S. citizens.

- Traveling with a U.S. passport. A U.S passport enables you to get assistance from the U.S. government when overseas, if necessary.

- Bringing family members to the U.S. U.S. citizens generally get priority when petitioning to bring family members permanently to this country.

- Obtaining citizenship for children born abroad. In most cases, a child born abroad to a U.S. citizen is automatically a U.S. citizen.

- Becoming eligible for federal jobs. Certain jobs with government agencies require U.S. citizenship.

- Becoming an elected official. Many elected offices in this country require U.S. citizenship.

- Meeting tax requirements. Tax requirements may be different for U.S. citizens and permanent residents.

- Keeping your residency. A U.S. citizen's right to remain in the United States cannot be taken away.

- Becoming eligible for federal grants and scholarships. Many financial aid grants, including college scholarships and funds given by the government for specific purposes, are available only to U.S. citizens.

- Obtaining government benefits. Some government benefits are available only to U.S. citizens.

Naturalization: Becoming a Citizen

The process of becoming a U.S. citizen is called "naturalization." You can apply for naturalization once you meet the following requirements:

- Live in the U.S. for at least 5 years as a permanent resident (or 3 years if married to and living with a U.S. citizen).

- Be present in the U.S. for at least 30 months out of the past 5 years (or 18 months out of the past 3 years if married to and living with a U.S. citizen).

- Live within a state or district for at least 3 months before you apply.

You may have to follow different rules if:

- You, or your deceased parent, spouse, or child, have served in the U.S. Armed Forces.

- You are a U.S. national.

- You obtained permanent residence through the 1986 amnesty law.

- You are a refugee or asylee.

- You have a U.S. citizen spouse who is regularly stationed abroad.

- You lost U.S. citizenship under prior law because of marriage to a non-citizen.

- You are an employee of certain types of companies or nonprofit organizations.

Consult A Guide to Naturalization for more information. You may also wish to consult an immigration attorney or other qualified professional.

GETTING NATURALIZATION INFORMATION

People 18 years or older who want to become citizens should get Form M-476, A Guide to Naturalization. This guide has important information on the requirements for naturalization. It also describes the forms you will need to begin the naturalization process.

To see if you are eligible to apply for naturalization, see Form M-480, Naturalization Eligibility Worksheet, at the end of A Guide to Naturalization. Use Form N-400 to apply for naturalization. There is a fee to file Form N-400.

To get Forms M-476, M-480, and N-400, call the USCIS Forms Line at 1-800-870-3676 or get them from http://www.uscis.gov.

Requirements for Naturalization

The general requirements for naturalization are:

1. Live in the U.S. as a permanent resident for a specific amount of time (Continuous Residence).

2. Be present in the U.S. for specific time periods (Physical Presence).

3. Spend specific amounts of time in your state or district (Time in District or State).

4. Behave in a legal and acceptable manner (Good Moral Character).

5. Know English and information about U.S. history and government (English and Civics).

6. Understand and accept the principles of the U.S. Constitution (Attachment to the Constitution).

MAINTAINING CONTINUOUS RESIDENCE (CR) AS A PERMANENT RESIDENT

If you leave the U.S. for:	Your CR status is:	To keep your status you must:
More than 6 months	Possibly broken	Prove that you continued to live, work, and/or have ties to the U.S. e.g., paid taxes) while you were away.
More than 1 year	Broken	In most cases, you must begin your continuous residence over. Apply for a re-entry permit before you leave if you plan to return to the U.S. as a permanent resident.

1. Continuous Residence

"Continuous residence" means that you must live in the U.S. as a permanent resident for a certain period of time. Most people must be permanent residents in continuous residence for 5 years (or 3 years if married to a U.S. citizen) before they can begin the naturalization process. For refugees, this means 5 years from the date you arrived in the U.S., which is usually the date you obtained permanent resident status. For those granted asylum status in the U.S., this period begins 1 year before you got permanent resident status. The date on your Permanent Resident Card is the date your 5 years begins. If you leave the United States for a long period of time, usually 6 months or more, you may "break" your continuous residence.

PRESERVING YOUR RESIDENCE FOR NATURALIZATION PURPOSES: EXEMPTIONS FOR 1-YEAR ABSENCES

If you work for the U.S. government, a recognized U.S. research institution, or certain U.S. corporations, or if you are a member of the clergy serving abroad, you may be able to preserve your continuous residence if you:

1. Have been physically present and living in the U.S. without leaving for at least one year after becoming a permanent resident.

2. Submit Form N-470, Application to Preserve Residence for Naturalization Purposes, before you have been outside the U.S. for one year. There is a fee to file Form N-470.

For more information, contact the USCIS Forms Line at: 1-800-870-3676 and ask for Form N-470, Application to Preserve Residence for Naturalization Purposes. You can also get the form on the USCIS website at http://uscis.gov/graphics/formsfee/forms/n-470.htm.

If you leave the United States for 1 year or longer, you may be able to return if you have a re-entry permit. You should apply for this re-entry permit before you depart the United States. See page 10 for information on how to apply for a re-entry permit. In most cases, none of the time you were in the United States before you left the country will count toward your time in continuous residence. This means that you will need to begin your continuous residence again after you return to the United States, and you may have to wait up to 4 years and 1 day before you can apply for naturalization.   • TIP: A re-entry permit (Form I-131) and the Application to Preserve Residence for Naturalization Purposes (Form N-470) are not the same. A re-entry permit lets you re-enter the U.S. as a permanent resident if you have been outside of the U.S. for more than 12 months. Form N-470 lets certain people maintain their continuous residence for naturalization purposes if they will be outside the U.S. for more than 12 months.

EXEMPTIONS FOR MILITARY PERSONNEL

If you are on active-duty status or were recently discharged from the U.S. Armed Forces, the continuous residence and physical presence requirements may not apply to you. You can find more information in the M-599 Naturalization Information for Military Personnel brochure. Every military base should have a point-of-contact to handle your naturalization application and certify a Form N-426, Request for Certification of Military or Naval Service. You must submit Form N-426 with your application forms. To get the forms you need, call the USCIS Forms Line at: 1-800-870-3676 and ask for the Military Packet. You can find the M-599 and Form N-426 at http://www.uscis.gov.

Be aware that absences from the United States while your naturalization application is pending could cause problems with your eligibility, especially if you accept employment abroad.

2. Physical Presence in the United States

"Physical presence" means that you actually have been present in the United States. If you are a permanent resident at least 18 years old, you must be physically present in the United States for at least 30 months during the last 5 years (or 18 months during the last 3 years, if married to a U.S. citizen) before you apply for naturalization.

"PHYSICAL PRESENCE"

Q: What is the difference between "physical presence" and "continuous residence"?

A: "Physical presence" is the total days you were inside the United States and does not include the time you spend outside the U.S. Each day you spend outside the U.S. takes away from your 'physical presence' total. If you are away from the U.S. for long periods of time or if you take many short trips outside the U.S., you may not meet your "physical presence" requirement. To count your "physical presence" time, you should add together all the time you have been in the United States. Then subtract all trips you have taken outside the United States. This includes short trips to Canada and Mexico. For example, if you go to Mexico for a weekend, you must include the trip when counting how many days you spent out of the country.

"Continuous residence" is the total time you have resided as a permanent resident in the United States before applying for naturalization. If you spend too much time outside the United States during a single trip, you may break your "continuous residence."

3. Time as a Resident in District or State

Most people must live in the district or state where they apply for naturalization for at least 3 months. Students can apply for naturalization either where they go to school or where their family lives (if they depend on their parents for support).

4. Good Moral Character

To be eligible for naturalization, you must be a person of good moral character. A person is not considered to be of "good moral character" if they commit certain crimes during the 5 years before they apply for naturalization or if they lie during their naturalization interview.

BEHAVIORS THAT MIGHT SHOW A LACK OF GOOD MORAL CHARACTER

- Drunk driving or being drunk most of the time.

- Illegal gambling.

- Prostitution.

- Lying to gain immigration benefits.

- Failing to pay court-ordered child support.

- Committing terrorist acts.

- Persecuting someone because of race, religion, national origin, political opinion, or social group.

If you commit some specific crimes, you can never become a U.S. citizen and will probably be removed from the country. These crimes are called "bars" to naturalization. Crimes called "aggravated felonies" (if committed on or after November 29, 1990), including: murder, rape, sexual abuse of a child, violent assault, treason, and trafficking in drugs, firearms, or people are some examples of permanent bars to naturalization. In most cases, immigrants who were exempted or discharged from serving in the U.S. Armed Forces because they were immigrants and immigrants who deserted from the U.S. Armed Forces are also permanently barred from U.S.citizenship.

You also may be denied citizenship if you behave in other ways that show you lack good moral character.

- 2 or more crimes with combined sentences of 5 years or more.

- Violating controlled substance laws (e.g., using or selling illegal drugs).

- Spending 180 days or more during the past 5 years in jail or prison.

Report any crimes that you committed when you apply for naturalization. This includes crimes removed from your record or committed before your 18th birthday. If you do not tell USCIS about them, you may be denied citizenship and you could be prosecuted.

5. English and Civics

Other crimes are temporary bars to naturalization. Temporary bars usually prevent you from becoming a citizen for up to 5 years after you commit the crime. These include:

- Any crime against a person with intent to harm.

- Any crime against property or the government involving fraud.

In general, you must show that you can read, write, and speak basic English. You also must have a basic knowledge of U.S. history and government (also known as "civics"). You will be required to pass a test of English and a test of civics to prove your knowledge.

Many schools and community organizations help people prepare for their citizenship tests. You can find examples of test questions in A Guide to Naturalization. You can get materials to help you study for these tests and practice tests on the USCIS website at http:// uscis. gov/graphics/services/natz/require.htm.

6. Attachment to the Constitution

You must be willing to support and defend the United States and its Constitution. You declare your "attachment" or loyalty to the United States and the Constitution when you take the Oath of Allegiance. You become a U.S. citizen when you take the Oath of Allegiance.

People who show they have a physical or developmental disability that makes them unable to understand the meaning of the oath do not have to take the Oath of Allegiance.

If you have a pending naturalization application and you move, you must notify USCIS of your new address. You can call 1-800-375-5283 to report your new address. You must also file Form AR-1 1 with DHS. See page 12 for instructions.

Naturalization Ceremonies

If USCIS approves your application for naturalization, you must attend a ceremony and take the Oath of Allegiance. USCIS will send you a Form N-445,

Notice of Naturalization Oath Ceremony, to tell you the time and date of your ceremony. You must complete this form and bring it to your ceremony.

If you cannot go to your ceremony, you can reschedule your ceremony. To reschedule, you must return Form N-445 to your local USCIS office along with a letter explaining why you cannot attend the ceremony.

You will return your Permanent Resident Card to USCIS when you check in at the Oath ceremony. You will no longer need your card because you will get a Certificate of Naturalization at the ceremony.